DETOUR

DETOUR

Grace H. Kaiser

Good Books

Intercourse, Pennsylvania 17534

Published by Good Books, Intercourse, PA 17534

Design by Dawn J. Ranck

Cover illustration by Denny Bond

DETOUR

Copyright © 1990 by Grace H. Kaiser

International Standard Book Number: 1-56148-062-2

Library of Congress Card Catalog Number: 90-3361

Library of Congress Cataloging-in-Publication Data

Kaiser, Grace H.
    Detour / Grace H. Kaiser.
      p.   cm.
    ISBN 1-56148-062-2 : $9.95
     1. Kaiser, Grace H.—Health.   2. Obstetricians—Pennsylvania—Lancaster County—
Biography.   3. Gynecologists—Pennsylvania—Lancaster County—Biography.   4. Osteopaths—
Pennsylvania—Lancaster County—Biography.   5. Physically handicapped—Pennsylvania—
Lancaster County—Biography.   6. Amish—Pennsylvania—Lancaster County—Social life and
Customs.   I. Title.
RG76.K34A3   1990
618.2'0092—dc20
[B]
                                        90-3361
                                        CIP

This book is dedicated to my husband, to Peter who has picked me from the floor more times than I wish to remember, held my arm to guide me over places my legs could not walk alone. He prodded me when I became discouraged and remained by my side when many marriages would have been shattered by the sudden addition of a disabled mate.

These stories are true. Most names and places have been changed and relocated. In several chapters experiences have been combined to create a continuous story. The excerpts from Peter's journal are printed as he wrote them.

Table of Contents

"In the middle of the journey of our life I came to myself within a dark wood where the straight way was lost."

Dante
The Divine Comedy

1
Blizzard

People die in blizzards. Sometimes they get lost in the whirling frenzy and their frozen bodies lie in an isolated furrow or among corn stubble and are not found until the snow melts.

Growing up in eastern Pennsylvania, I had watched blizzards from behind window panes, in the comfort of warm rooms but had never seen a winter snowstorm unleashed on Lancaster County. Never had it been my responsibility to clash with this adversary. It would happen some day, and the knowledge that my rural patients expected their doctor to meet any villainous weather chilled me as snowflakes sifted into the barren pear tree and blew against mounded rose bushes. I dreaded snowstorms.

Blizzards hold awesome terror and beauty in their majestic power. Stories of people lost in drifts, frozen stiff, fingers and toes turning black and falling off, were among Grandfather's retold legends. Until his death, he relived the blizzard of 1888 in vivid detail at each winter's first flakes.

In the gray dusk Pete and I watched snowflakes of a predicted blizzard pirouette across our brown barn in fairy dances. They swirled against the faded wooden garage and dropped exhausted into an infant drift fingering its way across the drive.

My husband put an arm around me. "I'm sure glad it's Friday and

I don't have to think about leaving the house until Monday," he said, shivering at the thought.

By bedtime only a little muffled traffic traveled New Holland's streets. The night was occasionally punctuated by a broken tire chain thumping a fender in sharp rhythm as some adventuresome soul braved the snowy night. The streetlight across Main Street was a milky blur. Icy blasts churned drifted snow with the falling flakes. It blew down the fireplace chimney, sending ashes into the living room. The storm wailed through the naked elm trees like sirens.

"Hope all my pregnant women stay quiet," I said at bedtime, pulling my nightgown over my head. "I've stocked up on bread and milk like everybody else. If the storm doesn't take down the electric lines, we'll be warm and fed. I got out the campstove and some candles, just in case." The quilts pulled around my neck gave a warm safe feeling.

Pallid morning showed no letup. Spruce trees behind the house sagged with vanilla frosting. Our driveway was closed. An occasional truck drove the street. It was a day to crawl into a warm hole, curl up and watch others flounder in the drifts.

As positive as an engraved invitation, the telephone rang, requesting my presence at a birthing. No R.S.V.P. possible.

"Emma'll be needin' ya after while," Marvin Weaver said. "No hurry but in this weather ya better start out. Her labor ain't too strong yet."

Emma, why Emma, far out in the country? Why Emma, tenth pregnancy, twins the last time, maybe trouble at this birthing? Could I even get to her? She would need a doctor, not a neighbor or husband substitute. It would be better for me to reach her for the planned home birth than try to get her out and end up in a snow-bank. "Your road open?" I asked.

"I think so, but not our lane. I'll meet ya at the highway with the tractor in an hour and bring you into the house. Okay?"

"Okay." But it was not okay. Neither my husband nor I owned a four-wheel drive. Even traveling in New Holland without it would be risky. The Weaver's serpentine lane followed along a tree-edged creek that caught wind and snow for nearly a mile. No other road in. I must have a 4 × 4. Last summer George Hoover, a block down Main Street, had offered his Jeep if I ever needed transportation in a storm. I had to use it.

Pete threw a shovel into the Jeep and sat beside George. I took my office nurse Anna Good with us. She would be an extra pair of hands, dressing the baby and enjoying the emotional high that birthing a baby gives the participants. Wrapped in blue wool hat, heavy red coat and swathed in a green plaid muffler, Anna squeezed in beside me on the back seat. Every time we opened the Jeep's door or met an icy blast, cold wind stung our faces and squinted our eyes. I was glad that I did not have to fight the blizzard alone.

Certain that the shortcut back roads through the farmlands would be drifted shut, we drove to Blue Ball and west. The blowing snow mingled with the new flakes obscuring roads, fences and ditches. The landscape melted together in an opaque distorted haze.

George knew that the road lay between telephone poles on one roadbank and electric poles on the other. He steered down the middle hoping we met no other cars navigating the same course. Our tire chains grabbed the snow sending us through drifts we could not see until they flew over us like hurricane waves crashing the bow of a ship. At times we moved ahead in a straight line; sometimes we slid drunkenly along the crown of the road.

Passing through crossroad villages, houses stood out in blurred silhouettes, their gloomy windows dark sunken eyes. "Looks like we're coming into Hinkletown," George called from within the wrappings of a gray muffler. The vapor of his words rose in a steamy cloud.

Staring intently into the storm, we nearly missed Marvin waiting at the roadside. He jumped from his caterpillar tractor like a huge black bear charging from its winter den, shook snow from his coat and exhaled mist like a smokestack. "Glad you made it. Emma's fine yet. We'll hafta go through the fields. I'll break the way with the tractor." Snow dusted Marvin's long lashes and stubbled cheeks, closely framed by a black leather hat that fit over his ears and neck. He squinted through our open door. "Okay?"

"Yes," George agreed, slim shoulders shrinking deeper into his red mackinaw as a gust of cold wind rattled the Jeep's canvas roof. He pulled his brown wool cap over his ears, revved the engine and nodded to the bear.

"Follow me." Marvin kicked the tractor to loosen snow from his knee-high gum boots and heaved himself onto the caterpillar seat, grasping its control levers with hands clothed in bulky black gloves.

Off across the field. Sometimes stuck, backing up to churn forward, grinding in low gear, rushing forward, always the clanking tractor ahead, always snow in the wind and under our spinning, sliding wheels.

Halfway to the house we stopped, the Jeep engine roared, wheels whirling. "The transmission. Guess we tore the rear out." George moaned, rubbing his reddened beakish nose. "We're as far as we'll go."

Pete and George got out, tromping around in snow to their boot tops. We watched them mutter and gesture.

Marvin backed the tractor to the Jeep. "I'll take the women into the house on the tractor then we can see about your Jeep. It'll take two trips."

Powdery snow filled my boots as I stepped out of the Jeep to stand on the tractor hitch that last summer had coupled Marvin's plow. With one hand I clutched the black bag needed for Emma's delivery, the other gripped the tractor seat. We crept over the fields, the clanking caterpillar tracks braiding wide bands in the snow. Wind-driven flakes knifed my cheeks and blinded me. The only protection was behind Marvin. I was disoriented in the bland landscape, but Marvin knew his geography. Finally his snow-smudged red barn emerged through the white curtain. At the wire yard fence I dismounted onto a shoveled walk to the house. Marvin returned to fetch Anna.

The old stuccoed stone farmhouse took on a fresh clean face in its plaster of snow. Its dark shuttered windows looked like the black openings into ancient cliff dwellings.

At the kitchen door I shook snow from my corduroy slacks, took off my boots, knocked out the snow and entered stocking-footed. I warmed myself at the hot space heater. It felt like the best thing that had happened to me that day.

The room seemed filled with children. Mary and Barbara put dishes away into the cupboard. Their brother John, in a lounge chair, read a book. Three little boys played quietly with wooden cows and horses on the couch near the space heater that crackled with fresh coal. Twin brother and sister, the youngest children at four, crayoned a Sears catalogue at a long linoleum-covered table. All the boys wore work pants and blue shirts. Elva, the eldest, wore a white net cap, covering over hair combed into a bun at the nape of her neck. The little girls wore gingham dresses. Two older girls wore a cape and apron in the style of Old Order Mennonites.

Marvin Weaver's family belonged to a group of Mennonites that allowed tractors in the field but no modern conveniences in the house. A bucket of water pumped from the well sat with a long-handled dipper in the lead-lined dry sink.

For transportation Marvin and Emma rode in a horse-drawn black buggy on errands to Ephrata or New Holland. Every other Sunday they drove their horse to the frame church enclosed by wagon sheds, the cemetery and the highway. An iron pump poked through the scuffed grass of the gravel churchyard like a periscope.

Unmarried boys and girls rode bicycles everywhere. On Sunday afternoons they clustered on country roads like swarming bees. Men often biked on errands, but older women usually walked or harnessed a horse to wagon or buggy.

Elva, sixteen, was in charge of the Weaver kitchen. She poured hot cornmeal mush into pans at the brown enameled coal range. Several kettles whispered gentle steam, salivating bubbles that danced across the hot iron plates until they disappeared. She asked Eva, thirteen, to hang my snowy hooded coat behind the stove and Barbara to carry the mush into the washhouse. "Mom's in the bedroom." Her voice was soft. She nodded toward a closed door and blushed.

I pulled my boots back on and entered the bedroom. Its combed varnished trim was scuffed from years of habitation. Glare from the snow pierced white lace curtains and reflected on bare walls and peeling paper once bright with roses. Marvin's Sunday suit and several dresses hung from hangers and metal hooks on a board nailed against one wall. An antique bed, with high headboard and sleigh footboard, was spread with a plastic sheet and covered with a newspaper pad according to instructions. A wash basin sat on the matching oak dresser.

Emma paced the worn linoleum floor; her long muslin nightgown swayed around brown felt slippers as she moved toward the square brown space heater to turn warming baby clothes. "I stay in here to be away from the children," she said. The smile that wrinkled her jowled face assured me that she was in control of her labor. During a contraction she held her pendent abdomen, smiled again and pushed loose gray hair under her cap. "Not right away," she said. "But with this blizzard we thought you oughta start out in plentya time."

Anna came into the room, her face apple-red from the whipping snow of her tractor ride. "The men are out in the field digging and pulling the Jeep out." She laid a towel-wrapped pack of sterile clamps and scissors on a plank bottom chair, drew Pitocin into a syringe and checked the warming baby blankets.

Anna and I rocked in cushioned parlor chairs two hours, past noon dinner, while Emma labored. After one hour the men came into the kitchen, glad to be warm and out of the frigid relentless wind. Marvin checked on the bedroom progress frequently until time to stay with his wife during the birthing. George and Pete shed boots and coats and waited on the kitchen couch.

Over all my years of practice, if there was anything that impressed Pete about any of my patients, it was the quiet obedience and behavior of those ten Weaver children. Elva, with the help of her sisters, dished out a meal of mashed potatoes, fried sausage with gravy, home-canned string beans, fresh baked bread, applesauce, jars of peaches and chocolate cake. Marvin ate with them but the men on the couch declined. The meal finished, the boys went to feed the steers and open the lane with tractor and shovel. The girls cleaned the kitchen.

My concerns for Emma's birthing, our isolation should she hemorrhage or be unable to deliver, were unnecessary. When the patient finally stopped walking and agreed to lie down, birth was ten minutes away. With Emma's final push came a wet black-haired head, corrugated by pressure as it crowned the perineum, next a fat-cheeked face. I wiped away the flood of fluid and mucus from the baby's nose as it tumbled onto the bed. It coughed and cried but stopped when she felt the warmed blankets. Until the baby girl gave her first lusty cry, no one in the kitchen knew Emma's labor was over.

Anna and I cleaned up and packed up. The children in the kitchen filed into the bedroom to see their new sister. Each one held her a moment before we laid the baby beside Emma. Anna and I talked about the tedious trip home, wondering if the highway had been completely closed in the past hours.

"The boys opened the lane. The Jeep's okay," Pete said. "We were hung up on a drift with all the wheels spinning in the snow." He pulled on boots, hat and a bulky brown corduroy coat. He looked like an overstuffed chair. I interpreted the grin that spread over his round face as happiness in heading home.

"Son John says there's a snowplow waiting for ya at the end of the lane to help ya home," Marvin announced as we layered ourselves into the Jeep.

Before the birth we had seen through the bedroom windows that the snow had stopped and the sun come out. But I was not prepared for the dazzling, blinding brilliance. A breathless silence claimed the land. Snow drifts cast no shadows. Height and depth indistinguishable, the rolling fields and fence rows appeared level from one distant tree line to the next. The land was as unblemished as the newborn cuddled in Emma's arms. Until we reached the highway, the only sound was the winding churning creek and the Jeep engine, muted by the snow.

The snowplow driver hailed us, "Glad to see ya. Waited here in case ya had any emergency."

"Thank you," I said. The possibility always made me uneasy. "How long have you waited?"

"'Bout an hour. According to the radio, New Holland is completely isolated, declared a state of emergency." The driver climbed into the cinder-loaded dump truck. "Follow me. I'll take ya home." He gunned his engine, lowered the great V-blade and plowed east into the drifts of Route 322.

All the side roads were bank full with blizzard. As the plow sliced drift after drift, crimping white margins like the crinkled edge of a pie crust, we marveled that we had traveled this road four hours ago.

Nothing moved around us. Not even a crow skimmed the turquoise sky. Smug behind the carving plow, we debated how many days before farms on the horizon could travel their roads again, how many gallons of milk would be poured onto the ground before silver beetle milk trucks could suck out bulk tanks. A few herdsmen would haul milk cans by sleigh or wagon out to a plowed main road for pickup. By evening fences would be cut open and newly rutted field lanes packed by wagons and tractors on their way to the outside world. Tomorrow, Sunday services would be cancelled; Monday, the schools closed until buses could travel safely.

During blizzards snowplow drivers worked around the clock, exhausted but grateful for time-and-a-half and double-time tax money. Winters with too many snows depleted appropriations and made unhappy commissioners juggle funds.

Several miles west of Blue Ball, we met a black car hopelessly stuck in the ditch. When the plow stopped, two young men and two girls, clothed only in sweaters, nothing on their shoes, stepped out into hip-deep snow chattering that they had driven from Philadelphia to see what the blizzard on the radio was like. Philadelphia and Downingtown had had only a dusting of snow. Pete and George, aided by the plow, pulled them from the drift and turned them back toward Downingtown. They followed our Jeep. Amazed at city people's foolishness, we shook our heads. No native would go without chains or snow tires scantily dressed into a snowstorm.

Through Blue Ball and along Route 23 into New Holland, heavily coated and gloved snow shovelers stopped digging out driveways to watch our parade behind the plow. Several pickups and cars followed us to our house, then to George's edge of town where the plow turned back to Blue Ball and eastward.

The tourists from Philadelphia may have considered the blizzard a winter picnic, but I was thankful that I had been able to reach Emma without freezing to death in a snowbank, that her delivery was uneventful, that the plow had waited and brought us home.

The fireplace at 561 West Main Street felt as warm and friendly as the people helping each other through the snow. Life was good and would go on forever. I would retire when I was too old and feeble to practice. In my declining years I saw myself visiting former patients, rocking and chatting in their cozy farm kitchens. But fantasies are not truth.

2
Pizzicato

Even today I cannot believe that it all happened, that life without warning can dogleg so rapidly into an unpredictable direction.

"Never in a thousand years," I kept saying to friends who came to gaze over my hospital bedrails and offer condolences. "Never could I imagine myself disabled." Me, two-steps-at-a-time mother and doctor, vigorous and indefatigable.

Pete and I, with another couple, had chosen Starlight Campground to manage a square dance weekend reminiscent of the many we had conducted when we owned Spring Gulch Campground.

One final pizzicato and it was over. I was alive, but I could not move. Death had swooped down in a streak of orange light. Its searing talons had seized me, let go. Paralysis was immediate. I fell like a soggy scrub rag. The tent camper shook on impact. The floor was dark, cold against my cheek.

Only a second before I had looked over my shoulder to see what trapped my left leg as I slid along a bench behind the table. I reached for a sleeping bag on the far bunk. The light cord wrapped my left ankle, released.

Then the blow between the eyes. A fiery blaze. My legs and hips seemed to rise to an impossible right angle above my body before they drifted in phantom slow motion to a contorted tangle on the floor.

Pete's steps crunched gravel between the shower house and our campsite.

"Come in, Pete," I called. "I fell and really hurt myself."

My husband opened the camper door. "What happened?" He shone his flashlight over my limp body. "I heard the thump outside."

"Run your hands over my legs." I waited a moment. "Did you do it?"

"Yes, pinched them too."

"I didn't feel anything."

"Shine your light on my face. What is trickling from my nose?"

"Blood." Pete answered.

"Good." At impact my body had hurled against the edge of the bunk like a discus at full speed. My head felt as if it had been split open from the inside. I was sure that I had fractured my skull. If it were possible for clear fluid around the brain to leak through the nose after an injury, I was in bad trouble. I was a doctor. My diagnoses ran wild journeys. Where was my injury? What had happened?

"Don't let anyone touch me or move me," I told Pete. Survival could depend upon the way I was moved. We had driven Pete's van. No car phone. "Go down to the campground office and call the special ambulance from Community Hospital in Lancaster."

It was an ambulance equipped for trauma, heart attacks or other catastrophic emergencies. Specially trained paramedics stood by around the clock, ready to speed away in the ambulance parked outside the emergency room door. I wanted to be moved by experts.

"Okay. I'll get somebody to be with you until I get back." I heard Pete run to the campsite across the driveway and ask Mary Stoner to stay with me.

"Let's cover you with a blanket," Mary said. She stood outside the camper at my head while Pete hurried down the mountain. "Do you hurt anywhere?"

"No."

"Anything I can do for you?"

"No," I answered.

We did not speak much but I heard her breathing in the doorway.

Her feet grated on the gravel.

"Can they come? Were they out on a call?" I asked Pete when he returned. I pulled myself into consciousness.

"They're on the way. Twenty miles will take awhile, even for an ambulance," he said.

"Don't move me," I repeated to the volunteer ambulance crew from Brickerville who came to strap a collar around my neck by request of Lancaster's emergency room. They fastened the thick collar and stayed, with their ambulance, to assist if needed. Time hung in black limbo on the cold air. We waited. Hushed voices mumbled outside the camper. Shoes crunched stones as people shifted feet or came and went.

"Where's that ambulance?" I asked several times. Lost? No siren cut night's silent curtain. How long did I lie under the blanket in my underwear drifting in and out of consciousness? Even the beeper I wore in my bra was silent. I thought about the happy weekend we had planned.

Our first childless weekend in many years. Pete and I had driven twenty-five miles west into the Furnace Hills area. The velvet October air was heavy with the odor of dank earth, speckled with gold and amber falling leaves. The narrow road twisted beneath the forest canopy. At the campground we spiraled hairpin turns to a campsite overlooking miles of wrinkled calico hills, red and yellow maples, green pine and spruce and brown fall oaks.

We had opened our camper and searched for firewood that I used to cook steaks. Inside the camper Pete clamped an overhead light to a strut that supported the camper's top. He ran a cord down the side and over the bench to a socket.

Accustomed to several decades of child watching, there seemed little to say in the void of watchful discipline. In two years our last child would leave for college. I wondered what couples talked about after their children left home. What common bond held them together. Nothing broke the awkward silence as we prepared our campsite and dressed for the square dance.

Friday the thirteenth was nearly over when Pete and I drove up the hill after the dance in the recreation hall. We would lie in our sleeping bags, smell the moist woods, listen to leaves sift onto the canvas roof, perhaps hear an owl hoot through the trees.

Pete walked to the shower house. I took off my dress and crinoline petticoat. It would be nice to sleep with my husband on one bed instead of alone, separated by the table and benches. I slid along the bench behind the table, stretched to reach a sleeping bag on the far bunk when my foot caught in the light cord. It released, hurling me forward. I lay on the floor, waiting.

"Isn't the ambulance here yet?" I asked several times, rousing to consciousness. "Can you hear it coming?" Often I had waited beside a patient for the welcome cry of a siren.

At last a pale lament, like the night yowl of distant dogs, then the modulating whine until it became a scream. Finally, blinking red lights reflected into my dark corner.

"What a trip up this mountain. Couldn't make good time, even with the state police escorting us as far as the campground," the ambulance crew complained. They conferred, deciding on the best way to apply a backboard to a woman scrunched in a heap, wedged between a table leg and the back wall of the camper. "Relax," they reassured me. "We'll soon have you out."

A tent camper is no more than a cube on wheels. Floor space is scarce. Ours had two beds that unfolded over the ground when in use. Lying with my face against one metal corner, it was impossible to see anything. The bleeding from my nose had stopped. Muffled voices seemed far away. Most of the time I felt drowsy but responded "no" when asked if I was cold, felt any pain or had a headache.

Strong arms pushed straps under my body, securing me to the backboard. The ambulance attendants spoke to me as they worked, explaining each step. Later Pete told me that the canvas top of the camper was unsnapped and the table removed. The night air revived me like a splash of cold water as I was lifted over the edge of the trailer, turned on my back and carried to the ambulance. Its familiar medicinal odors, the green oxygen tank against the bulkhead, the blood pressure cuff on my arm were comforting. I felt safe.

The ride out of the campground was a trip down a corkscrew. No wonder the men on the ambulance complained about the curves. I conversed with the attendants, spoke over the intercom to Terri, emergency care specialist. "No, I can breathe fine," I answered when she asked about respirations in order to determine if my injury was high enough in the neck to affect the nerves that control breathing. She laughed at a patient who answered instead of the crew. During Terri's days as a medical student, she had been a guest in my home, traveled night's country roads and sped down bleak farm lanes with me as we raced to home births.

Lying in the camper, I had felt no pain. It began in the bouncing, vibrating, boxy ambulance. Every sensory nerve fiber seemed over-stimulated, stood on end, scoured raw with sandpaper. Each crack and seam in the road felt like a pothole, accentuating and intensify-ing my agony. Would we never reach the hospital? I was crying with agitation and pain when we backed up to the emergency room doors.

The emergency room was warm and comforting. I was sur-rounded by familiar walls and faces. Often I had passed through these doors with patients on a rush trip to surgery or the delivery room.

At 2:00 a.m. I wondered if the orthopedic surgeon, whom I knew, and the strange neurosurgeon from General Hospital across town were called from bed or dragged away from a party . It was good to see them, but their presence prior to tests or X rays confirmed my conviction that this injury was serious, even life threatening. I was carefully undressed and gowned for x-ray.

The nurse handed Pete my beeper before she scissored my bra up the front. Men wore beepers on their belts, but I had no belt or pockets. Once at a banquet I had carried it in my purse and did not hear its signal. My answering service had been frantic, trying to locate me for a patient in labor. Mid-bra against the skin was the best place.

Strangers stared the first time they heard the beep, watching me dive and grope to find the "off" button. I pretended that mine was accepted procedure and the gawker unconventional. One Sunday morning during the sermon our minister mistook my beeper for the signal to turn his cassette over as he taped his sermon for shut-ins. I wore it at the Starlight weekend in case a woman began labor.

Except for the ride on the litter, taking the X rays remains hazy. Back in the emergency room both physicians examined, pinched, squeezed, pricked my legs and body up to my head. I could not move my arms or lift a finger. My legs did not respond when I tried to bend the knees or flex a foot.

"Nothing fractured or dislocated," the doctors said. "Wiggle your toes." On the left foot nothing happened. The big toe on the right foot answered with the slightest movement, a banner too heavy for the air. I lifted my head to watch its feeble attempt.

"Good, wonderful," the orthopedist said. "She doesn't need me. I might as well go home."

"You'll get it back again," the neurosurgeon said, meaning mobility. He smiled. "We'll send you upstairs. I'll write orders and keep tabs on you."

"How long before I can get back to the office?" I asked, seeing in my mind the long list of women who would need me the next months. Who would care for Emma Hoover confined to bed in Vogansville, threatening to deliver a seven-month baby? Annie Stoltzfus from White Horse would soon birth twins. I thought of Martha Martin and all the other women who depended on me to drop whatever I was doing and go to their bedsides when their husbands phoned. Many patients had never had another doctor deliver them. Next week's appointments must be cancelled. But how? Some people used public telephones or their neighbor's. It would require careful planning, and someone to cover my practice until I could work again. With all the farm accidents in twenty-eight years of practice, I had seen no spinal-cord-injured patients, but remembering medical school classes, I knew it would require weeks to recover.

"Nine months to a year," the doctor answered.

I hung my hope and future on his promise. Life without a list of women due to deliver babies, without office appointments, away from telephone or beeper was inconceivable. From that moment the days, weeks, months, were a countdown toward nine.

Nine months. A long time. Occasional summer camping trips of four weeks always seemed endless.

A medical practice is necessarily a business. While the emergency room nurse prepared me for bed, I gave Pete instructions. Office nurse Edie would not be needed. Betts could continue to answer the phone, keep records and reroute patients to other doctors until I returned to the office next summer.

"No use paying for a car phone," I said. "Might as well take it out.

Return the beeper to Ephrata too. Tell Patsy at the answering service who will cover my practice."

The treatment and prognosis of spinal cord injuries were as foreign to me as the fevers and cures of deepest Africa. My longest hospital stay had been a routine five postpartum days. Nine months was not the rest of my life. I resolved to do whatever was needed to hammer down that time. I would accept the verdict, be a model patient, focusing on the promise and filled with hope.

"You'll get it back. Nine months to a year." I tatooed these words into my brain, read and reread them through winter and spring into summer. I had asked an honest question. Deception was unbelievable.

I was comforted by the thought that nine months was not forever. Our children were grown and did not need me. The next months would not be easy, but I could resume my practice and continue life as before. Resigned to accept my injury, I resolved to shorten the nine months. Sleep came easily.

3

Hospital Daze

Saturday, first hospital day after the accident, was distorted. Like Alice in Wonderland, I had passed through the mirror. The world appeared mangled. Instead of standing beside the bed giving orders, I was in it, even basic self-care impossible. The rigid handle on the door had more motion than I as it swung open and shut all day with nurses recording vital signs, giving cortisone, turning me every two hours. They checked IVs and the Foley catheter that drained my bladder.

While the last twelve years of my twenty-eight-year rural practice had been limited to obstetrics, the rest of medicine had jetted into new territory. The procedures on this hospital wing were a trip into a foreign land. The landscape and its people cast strange shadows. New phrases, letters and abbreviations rolled off tongues as rapidly as the nurses moving room to room.

My hands seemed alien when the nurse lifted them at my morning bath. They were like the clawed ones that grope the edges of caskets in horror movies. Without nerve supply, the muscles had collapsed against the bones like wilted flowers hugging their stems. Even the tortuous blue veins had disappeared. The palms were flat, cupless, as the nurse stretched out spastic fingers to wipe hands insensitive and numb. The hand resumed fist position when released.

The hands, wrists and arms that had delivered several thousand babies, changed flat tires along country roads, thrown my children over one shoulder and down the other looked as if I had been on a six-week fast.

Only last week I had jogged New Holland streets on crisp October evenings. Now my legs seemed lifeless, vericosities sunken into collapsed muscles. "My legs feel ice cold," I said.

"Your legs are toasty warm," the nurse assured me. "Just yell if you want anything. We're right across the hall." Pressing a call button was impossible. Screaming "nurse" until one heard me was demeaning. It reminded me of withered, toothless, disoriented elderly patients restrained in bed and chair calling pitifully for nurse and family.

My husband hung a clay windchime above my head. I lifted my head and grasped the leather thong in my teeth, but it had to hang inches above my face. On the second day I pulled too hard. The chime fell, hit me on the head, bounced to the floor and broke. I resigned myself to shouting.

"What name do you want us to call you?" the nurse asked the routine question on admission.

Immobility was new, but inside lived a member of the medical staff. I had always been addressed as Doctor Kaiser. Why should I demand less respect than when I walked the halls and wrote orders? Little remained other than my name. "Doctor Kaiser," I answered.

When I requested a mirror, I saw a swollen nose between puffy black-and-blue eyes. "Who won the fight?" the nurse asked. Laughing hurt my head. A small towel rolled under my neck relieved pain where the vertebrae hyper-extended as I fell.

Saturday afternoon my wedding band felt tight as my fingers began to swell. A nurse soaped, wiggled and pulled to work it over the thickened knuckle.

A nurse checking vital signs Saturday evening aroused me from heavy sleep. "What is your normal pulse?" Stuporous, I told her that it was usually about eighty. Within minutes she returned with Doctor Jack, the house physician. I had known him as he traveled through medical school, internship and residency. Now he was in charge of me.

"What is it?" I asked, too groggy to open my eyes.

"Thirty-five," he said.

"It's never been that low before." After two atropine injections my heart rate improved and I became alert.

That first weekend the muscle spasms began. Leg muscles contracted in knots like those that had made me pace the floor when calcium levels fell during pregnancies. This time I could not walk or rub them. My calcium was normal. I did not know that the uncontrollable jerks were due to interruption of cord impulses caused by my injury. The spasms were not painful but my jumping legs shook my body. Antispasmotics had little effect.

Intermittent impulses, charges of electricity, began to fly down my arms and legs. They zipped to the tips of fingers and toes in bursts of burning sparks, like exploding sky rockets on July Fourth.

If only someone had explained that spasms were a part of spinal cord injuries, that I would be a spastic the rest of my life, I would have understood and known what to expect. I thought of chickens beheaded for Sunday dinner on my childhood farm. They had twitched and jumped after Grandfather's axe chopped off their heads. Little of my symptoms or recovery was discussed with me. Time unraveled the story of my accident and what it meant.

If I as a physician did not know what to expect, I have often wondered how other patients survive tragic accidents. My medical background was often an asset in recovery, but the experience was new to me.

The spinal cord is like a cable of kite strings running downward inside the vertebral column, from a multitude of kite nuclei in the brain. At various levels between the vertebrae, dendrite fibers, the kite strings, leave the cord to end in muscles and organs. The purpose of the cord, protected by the vertebrae and wrapped in a myelin sheath, is conduction of impulses between fiber endings and the nuclei in the brain. If cut, these fibers of the central nervous system never regenerate, nor can they be reconnected. Research has shown where and how given impulses travel but has not been able to discover how to repair cut pathways. Even a bruise of the cord can damage delicate tracts forever.

Mine was a bruise of the cord. There was no way to determine the amount of residual destruction or how much recovery to expect. Physical examination determined the level of injury to be at the seventh cervical vertebra.

The quadriplegic effect of my incomplete cord injury was the same as a complete one in which the spinal cord is severed—paralysis from neck to toes. The amount of possible recovery was unknown. Circulation to the cord is poor, healing slowly.

Slowly. Lying in bed, nine months sounded endless. I put myself in limbo until recovered, determined to be a model patient, do everything possible to return to practice sooner, make this detour as short as possible.

I had always regarded the handicapped with curiosity, pity and misunderstanding, distanced myself from them. No one in our family had been disabled or admitted to anything other than the discomforts of arthritis and old age. We prided good health, stamina and an invulnerability passed from generation to generation.

"Never in a thousand years could I have imagined myself disabled." I repeated this over and over to physicians and hospital staff who stopped to visit.

A physician friend planted the seed, "Now you can write a book. Your country experiences would make interesting reading."

"Me. Write a book! Don't be foolish, Hal." I laughed. "I can't even hold a pencil. Besides I don't know how to write." How could he be serious?

"Use a tape recorder," he said, as if covering the germ with earth and tamping it down.

Germination and harvest would be several years away but the words remained. I agonized over my fate. So much had been plundered. Write a book! Ridiculous. Never. Where was justice if fate had plucked me from essential work among my patients in order to write a book? The idea was ludicrous. Every day's total effort lay in recovery, in one shaft of light, therapy.

Therapy began the first Monday morning when the hospital cranked into full motion after the weekend. Cynthia, head of Occupational Therapy, came to my room to mold and rivet fleece-lined splints that held my hands in a semi-flexed position. Lamb's wool lined the splints fitting my calves, behind the heels and under the feet. Arms and legs fastened into the splints with velcro, I felt like a turkey dressed for an oven. The splints were part of me for more than six months, except during baths or therapy.

And then Joe came, slipping into view on crepe-soled shoes. "I'm from physiotherapy," he said. "Let's see what you can do." He poked, tapped and tested muscles. When he flexed my legs, I could kick them straight. They felt like sodden cold logs, but it was wonderful to know that some motion remained. Joe assured me that my legs were warm, but they had no feeling and seemed as frigid and hard as glacial ice.

My therapist was a clean shaven, apple cheeked, freckled, hammered-down, red headed, rotund Santa, built like a wrestler. His marble facade hid a temper that forged more conflicts than he often bargained for. He dressed neatly in tee shirt and creased pants. When supervising a patient's therapy, he pushed to the limit. He knew when to cajole, scold or compliment, to make a patient take one more step with crutches or walker, to raise an arm a bit higher. Joe demanded the most effort I could give. He became kind and understanding when I exhausted. If I felt down, he bragged about badgering his mother into washing his car or laundry. He boasted about girl friends. I enjoyed the entertainment which contained only a whiff of distorted truth.

Joe came to my room twice each day to make me use muscles I could not feel move. He felt minuscule responses when I attempted to use fingers, feet and limbs. "He's my ticket out of this hospital," I told Hal one day. I cooperated and tried to do everything asked of me. Each week muscles strengthened until mobility was perceptible.

Misery arrived the second week with a custom-fitted Philadelphia collar. It put pressure against my jaw making conversation difficult. The contraption was torture. At first I wore the collar all day, later only when upright. It allowed me to sit up and be removed from the bed. After ten days it was discontinued.

The collar did permit me to go to the gym for therapy. The porter moved me by litter to the only unfamiliar room in the hospital. Enroute between X ray and laboratory I had never taken time to see the mass of tubs, bars and exercise equipment. When we had enlarged the hospital, the physiatrist, physician in charge of physiotherapy, had risen in committee meetings to fight for space and equipment, but I never thought of the gym except for the valuable amount of hospital space it utilized. Now it was my life.

After two weeks in bed I was strapped to the tilt table to determine tolerance to erect posture. When I no longer became light-headed or had blood pressure changes, I graduated to a wheelchair.

One day Joe and several assistants braced my legs, locked the wheelchair before parallel bars and cinched a heavy webbed belt around my waist. "Stand up."

I rebelled. "No, I can't. My knees will buckle. My legs. I'll fall." Cold spindly tree-limb legs could not support me. The tile floor looked far below and hard. "Don't make me stand. No. No."

"If your knees buckle, you'll be on the floor. Let's go." Joe took a deep breath, grabbed the belt, watching my legs. He pulled me to my feet. "Keep your knees stiff."

My arms dangled, unable to hold the bars and prevent falling. I looked down. My knees had not collapsed. How long would Joe make me stand? He gripped the strap that balanced me. I felt like the Tower of Pisa, forgot to breathe.

"Now, take a step," Joe commanded.

"A what?" One step. Slowly I raised the right foot and slid it forward a few inches. Walking was not as I remembered. Concentrate. Remember to breathe. The left foot slid gingerly beside the right, then the right again. Three steps. Joe let me sink slowly into the chair an assistant had moved behind us. I was exhausted but ecstatic. I had walked.

Joe shrugged his shoulders. "It was okay." But I knew by his crooked smile and the spark in his eyes that he was pleased.

Within a week I walked ten then fifteen steps, watching my feet move between the parallel bars without feeling the floor. It was like walking on the stilts Father made when I was twelve. My feet had clumped everywhere that summer, rarely touching the ground.

It was only mid-November. I knew that July would find me fully recovered, back in my office and chasing storks again. "I'll walk by Thanksgiving, run by Christmas," I bragged to the neurosurgeon at his next visit. His response was a look I could not interpret. Did he doubt me?

Learning to walk was a small part of therapy. Pushing my limp body into a bathing suit for water exercise in the Hubbard Tank was like stuffing a rag doll into a dress shrunken three sizes too small. I could help by lifting my hips from the mattress but despite the loss of several pounds there seemed to be too much of me. Tugging off the wet suit was as difficult. Everytime I went to the gym, the retention catheter had to be connected and disconnected from the leg bag.

The Hubbard Tank rested in the gym floor. Therapy in its warmed water was worth the bathing suit struggle. Joe in swim trunks waited in the tank as I was lowered by hydraulic crane on a special litter. The buoyancy of water increased the range of motion when I flexed and extended fingers, arms, feet and legs. I could walk better in the tank. Joe wore a crazy plastic hat the day the photographer took pictures for the hospital newsletter.

I had worked at a swimming pool during medical school days, taught swimming and was not afraid of the water despite Joe's frequent threats to dunk me. The sessions in the water were a welcome break in routine, but I returned to bed fatigued and slept until supper.

The gym was a fascinating place, full of varied activity. Out-patients and in-patients learned to walk after strokes or amputations. Patients came for burn therapy. Men and women lined up in wheel-chairs for whirlpools or practiced using crutches. Every day was new and busy.

Monday through Friday were scheduled morning and afternoon visits to physiotherapy. Each day I spent one hour after lunch in Occupational Therapy, strengthening hands and fingers by placing pegs in holes, stacking cones as high as I could reach. Twice a day I was lifted into a wheelchair, and Doris the porter wheeled me to the gym. On Saturday one therapist worked with urgent cases, and I went to the gym only once.

Everywhere someone had to pick me up, set me down. I was balanced with pillows, turned, dressed and fed. "I feel like a sack of potatoes," I told Joe, remembering how Father shook 100-pound bags to settle knobby spuds, how he lugged and dragged them from corner to corner. They stayed wherever he put them. "I'm worth-less," I complained.

The day I looked into the gym's full-length mirror, I saw a bulky sack. Gym patients wore a front-tied billowing hospital gown over the gown worn in bed. I wore no bra or underwear. The gowns dangled from my shoulders like windless sails flapping the yardarms of an ancient ship. A woman's hospital hair style, arranged by her pillow, is "bird nest." The mirror reflected a sagging lumpy gunnysack, voluminous beyond my 150 pounds and older than 54 years. Slumped into the wheelchair, I looked like a pathetic bag lady dragged from the streets and dressed in her shroud.

I could not believe the reflection. After three weeks only traces of the black eyes remained, but could I look that unkempt and dowdy? Back in my room, the nurse dialed the phone and held it while I called home. Pete brought slacks, bras, blouses, socks and shoes to the hospital. I wore them every day. Before I left my room a nurse combed my hair. I became a new person.

The nurses were caring and conscientious, but I required special attention. They tried to feed me before the food cooled, but there were other patients to feed. Morning bath and dressing had to be completed before Doris came to push me to the gym. Morning and evening a nurse gave range-of-motion exercises to fingers, hands, arms, toes and legs. When in bed nurses used a draw sheet to turn me every two hours, buttressing my back with pillows. Despite concerned nursing care, the skin over my sacrum broke down and would not heal. Every nursing shift had its own remedy. Having no sensory perception, I was the worst enemy by lying on my back, the only position which relieved the relentless leg spasms.

Particularly until the dried blood from my nose was gone, having a nurse hold a tissue for nose blowing was a most uncomfortable part of care. I remembered my toddlers rolling their heads and squirming out of grasp. Teeth brushing was another annoying event. The toothbrush always seemed too hard, the paste too much, the pressure too light. It was more like a peppermint fist in my mouth.

Many nurses were familiar for their care to Mother two years before, Father last spring when each of them had been on this floor. The familiar faces and visitors relieved my trips into chasms of uselessness and depression that seemed bottomless. Often I felt as empty as Monday's church.

Nurse friends from the obstetrical floor stopped frequently. They brought gifts of perfume, lotion, kitchen crafts or crocheted bed socks. Best of all they carried departmental chitchat and news of my patients delivered by substitute doctors. They carried back my best wishes to the new mothers.

"Remember Mary and Emory?" Donna from obstetrics asked.

"How could I forget them?" I laughed remembering the couple.

"She delivered a boy during the night."

"Did she come in by ambulance this time?" I asked. "She sure caused a commotion when she came in for her last baby. Remember how surprised I was about the ambulance, how happy it made her?"

4
An Ambulance for Mary

"**A**mbulance?" I said, taking a step backward. "What ambulance?" Mary had called about 2:00 a.m. from a neighbor's phone. Hers had been disconnected because of unpaid bills. "She said she was in a hurry to have this baby and her husband would drive her in." Obstetricians have a knack for half-awake conversations. Had I missed something?

The scrub-suited nurse behind the labor room desk took a sip of black coffee and a deep breath, laid her pen on a page of nurse's notes and handed me Mary Jensen's chart. "Where did you find this patient? She's polished her nails and fixed her hair all morning. She's not in labor."

"Lives in a trailer court on Narvon Hill."

I thought about the hill between Blue Ball and Honeybrook and the trailer court on the edge of the Welsh Mountains. Big or little trailers, new and junky ones were poked between trees like fingers in a glove. I leafed Mary's chart.

"She seems like a poor soul." Nurse Cameron smiled, waiting to hear more.

"She is poor. Mousy and half afraid of her husband. Wouldn't be surprised if he knocks her around sometimes. She comes to me because I'm a woman and have had babies."

The nurse lifted another chart from the rack. "Mary's on welfare."

"Most families on that hill are. I get a lot of grief for the $35.00 Pennsylvania pays me for each baby delivered."

The nurse sipped again, swallowed, scratched her permed auburn head. "Night shift said Mary was a mess when the ambulance brought her in, hair hanging in strings, face dirty."

"But I still don't understand the ambulance. What happened? How is she now?"

Nurse Cameron insisted on completing her story, running a slim finger around the edge of her cup. "Night shift said she puffed and groaned when the ambulance crew brought her in, hugging a scruffy cardboard suitcase."

"They made her shower?"

The nurse nodded emphatically. "Then she got combed, put on makeup, quieted down."

"Guess Mary's never had much. She's from a family of twelve kids on the south side of the mountain. Father was a junk man. When he could find junk or felt like working. Between babies her mother cleaned houses for valley people."

The nurse added more coffee to her cup from an electric urn. "Looks like she's following her mother."

"Pregnant and married Emory at fifteen. A baby almost every year or so, except the time Emory was jailed for stealing chickens from a farm near Churchtown. Never saw her in my office wearing anything but a faded cotton dress and old sneakers. Always a kid hanging on her skirt."

"Not bad looking now she's fixed up. Doesn't talk much," Nurse Cameron said.

I nodded. "Answers when spoken to but doesn't look at you. Except for other trailer women, her social life is going to the store or the Methodist Sunday School on the other side of the mountain, when Emory takes her, which isn't often."

"The nurses on eleven to seven shift said her husband is no prize."

"He fits the lazy mountaineer picture. It's hard for welfare to dispute a bad back. Doesn't keep him from shuffling cards or rolling dice."

I opened the wide wooden door to Mary's labor room.

"Doctor, wait'ill you hear what happened to us on the way to the hospital." Mary sat up in bed. Vivid lipstick and large brown eyes accentuated a thin white face, lined by thirty years of hard times and children. She smiled, excited.

I warmed my stethoscope in my palm.

"We'd just started down the hill when our old car lost a wheel, rolled off in a clump of briers and elderberry bushes near the railroad bridge. And me with hard pains too." She pouted her lower lip, put on a mournful face.

"But an ambulance?" I placed a hand on her mounded abdomen and awaited a contraction.

"Get an ambulance," I told Emory. "I need an ambulance. But he grumbled that I didn't need none mor'an he did and told me to stop my beller'n. I told him iff'in he didn't get it I'd go sit in the middle of the road 'til somebody got one." Even in the shapeless faded hospital gown that hung everywhere and nowhere Mary looked fresh, hair neatly combed and held by a blue ribbon. She was better groomed than I had ever seen her.

I smothered a grin, imagined Mary swaying onto the double lines and dropping like a stone onto the middle of Route 322, loose skirts wrapped around cornstalk legs and bulging abdomen and clasping the scuffed cardboard suitcase. "That was a dangerous place to sit," I said. "What next?"

"Me rockin' an moanin' and Emory fussin' that all the houses on the hill was black as coal. No place to call. He just leaned against the hood of that rickety green Chevy hangin' on three wheels along the road. He was suckin' air through his teeth and spittin' on the black top so hard it splashed. Stubborn mule." She waved a hand in disgust.

The only movement under my hand was an occasional baby kick. The uterus remained relaxed. This new Mary interested me. She glowed with an "I'm as good as anybody" look. I thought of the timid woman I had just discussed with Nurse Cameron.

"Told him I'd have the baby there on Narvon Hill if he didn't get the ambulance. I had the last one fast. You recollect me birthin' Betsy?" Mary leaned forward awaiting my answer, her face as flushed as a ripe peach. She sensed my amusement.

I slid my stethoscope along Mary's chest trying to maintain a rock-rigid face. How could I forget the commotion she had caused at the hospital at her last delivery when she arrived ready to birth, all delivery rooms full and labor patients overflowing into hall alcoves?

The charge nurse had told me how Emory stomped down the hall as if the entire affair was too much disgraceful bother. Baby Betsy had arrived on a litter in the hall before Mary had time to remove dress or underwear. It happened so fast that she was lucky to even have an intern and nurse's aide with her. No wonder Mary panicked at the first twinge of labor.

"Did Emory call the ambulance last night?" I paused to listen to the unborn's steady heartbeat through the stethoscope.

"Him? No way. Said he'd go home and borrow Will Bosley's pickup but I knowed Will had the engine all apart and spread around yesterday, so it weren't runnin'. Emory just rubbed his greasy chin what needed shavin' and started home; said no ambulance would come without no doctor's say-so cause too many people used 'em fer hospital trips."

Mary stopped to watch me press my thumb against her ankle, testing it for fluid retention. She closed her eyes concentrating on her tale.

"He called me a cow and said he'd drag me off the road hisself iff'in his back weren't so bad. He wanted me to walk back home. He oughta have a baby. Him and his back." She opened mascaraed lids.

My nod fueled Mary's report. I thought of the many assistance checks paid due to back pain. "So Emory finally called the ambulance?" I motioned Mary to lift her gown so I could examine her abdomen. The acrid odor of violet cologne rose to hang between us.

"No. He said somebody drivin' the hill'd think me plastered or hit me like some cat warmin' its feet on the road. Finally when he seen I wouldn't get up, he said he'd call the ambulance, but a car come up the hill and a man stopped to ask if we needed help or if we was hurt."

Mary brushed away an imaginary tear with a fire-red finger. "The man could see me in pain and cryin' so he went back down the hill to a pay phone in Beartown and called Honeybrook ambulance. I told him to hurry. After that Emory sulked against a dented fender, said you'd think I never had no baby before. He lit a cigarette and snorted smoke outa his nose like a wild bull."

I shook my head, not insulting her with a smile, pictured Mary delivering on the middle of the road with only Emory and an unfortunate stranger.

Mary lifted broom-handle arms and pointed to several scratches from the macadam on her knotty elbows. "Then I rolled over on my hands and knees, got up and waited by the car."

I imagined a crew of Honeybrook's ambulance volunteers, a garage attendant and perhaps a farmer and the school nurse routed from their beds to pick up Mary below the crest of Narvon Hill. The ambulance had stood winking and blinking like a marquee on Times Square. The men unfolded a stretcher and rolled it to the derelict car to strap Mary, with her moans and groans, between clean blankets.

I pulled the sheet over Mary's chest and patted her arm, listening to her story.

"Coupla other cars stopped after that, but Emory jabbed his old blue flannel shirt into his saggy jeans and said help was comin', like he'd gone fer it. When the ambulance was stopped, he hiked his belt under his big belly and waved his fat arms around directin' traffic like he was a cop. Then he sat on the front seat while we come them twenty miles to Lancaster, siren splittin' cars off the road like firewood."

"You had quite a night," I said, finishing her examination. "You were lucky this baby was not as speedy as the last one. The ambulance ride was okay then?"

"Yeah." She smiled, pleased as a child at a birthday party. "Always wanted to ride in an ambulance, lights flashin' and siren screamin', people gettin' out of the way, lookin'." Mary became somber. "When's this baby comin'?"

"Not for awhile. False labor last night."

"I'm hungry. Can I have somethin' to eat? Can I go home? I oughta go home."

"Who is watching your children?" I asked.

"Emory. That's why I gotta get home. Emory! He jest lets the kids run over the neighborhood while he sets drinkin' beer. Hollers at them all day. Ain't good for kids. I'm wonderin' how he's doin' with Betsy, diapers, feedin' and all. I told him to take her to Janet in the next trailer, iff'in she's home. Baby's only eighteen months ya know. Men!" She threw up bony hands and fell against the pillow.

"Mary, you may go home as soon as you find a way to get there."

"Thank you doctor, thank ya. I wonder what my next trip'ill be like?"

"So do I, Mary," I said, closing the labor room door behind me, not knowing that it would be two weeks before her next admission. "So do I."

5

The Flipside

"The good part of a bad problem is on its other side. Turn it over," Velma Wenger said, catching up on a pile of mending after a cow stepped on her bare foot and restricted her to chair and bed for a week.

How that elf of a woman accomplished so much work in a day I never understood. No more than shoulder high to the snappy sorrel she harnessed and drove to town, she steered pigtailed daughters and tousle-headed mischievous sons through lawn mowing, garden planting, weeding and household chores. I never passed the Wenger house on a clear day that bedding did not air from upstairs windows, sheets and blankets lapping the shingled gray house like thirsty tongues.

In the area of the Wenger home, few people other than local farmers and a sprinkling of trailer residents traveled the isolated byways chopped into nubbins of dead-end side roads when farmland and forest were wolfed up by the Pennsylvania Turnpike. Over the more traveled routes, the turnpike spit out occasional bridges, loose irregular sutures in the wide gash across the state.

Sumac, wild blackberry and sassafras edged summer's narrow macadam backroads blending into unrestrained woods of maple, oak and poplar trees. Small stony farms wrangled from barbarous hills by former generations and an occasional one-room school or a trailer home interrupted the wilderness. The dank odor of under-brush and overgrowth clung to the air like the tenacled poison ivy groping fencerails and consuming telephone poles.

The language chatted over kitchen telephones of most Narvon RD#2 homes was Pennsylvania Dutch. Old Order Mennonite folks east of Bowmansville drove to church with horse and carriage. Some homes used electricity. Most families lit lanterns and kerosene lamps for light.

Velma and David Wenger could not support a growing family on their meager acres. Every morning a trailer neighbor took David to work with him on the assembly line of New Holland Machine Company. Evenings and weekends David tilled and battled his earth for corn, potatoes and hay.

Five miles back in the boondocks from the main highway, a roadside vegetable stand would have been as useful to Velma as a load of hay delivered to Lancaster City Hall. She shared her excesses with friends and neighbors.

When Velma drove her horse and carriage fourteen miles to my office, it was part of a journey to hunt clothing at Rubinson's and Trimmer's Department Stores, to have her horse shod, to buy tools or seed at Kauffman's Hardware. New Holland provided abundant horse sheds and hitching rails.

Velma never learned to walk. Her gait was a permanent trot. In my office she propelled her pre-schoolers onto waiting room chairs, distributed children's books from the table and laid out rules of good behavior.

"Can you use some cheese again?" Velma asked as she sat beside my desk. She extracted a plastic-wrapped pale full moon from a crinkled paper bag and laid it on the desk. "Cow's fresh, have to use up the milk." She pushed the cool cylinder toward me with small slim fingers, knowing my family hungered for her cheese. Her rennin came by mail order from the Midwest. David had made cheese presses the size of cereal bowls. Nothing bad could come from Velma's immaculate kitchen.

"Thank you," I said, already imagining the cheese's soft texture on a cracker, incisor marks in its pliant anatomy, soft curd nestled on my tongue. "I'll have to hide this in the refrigerator if I want any of it."

"Will you come to my house in January?" Velma asked, removing her small black bonnet. She wrinkled her petite face in smiles, azure eyes bright as a child's. I never refused her.

"Promise no snowstorms?" I thought of the miles between us wrapped in blizzard solitude, roads impassible, snow-blocked.

"No guarantees," she laughed, remembering the times I had straddled one-track ice ruts to reach her. Backroads could be closed a week. Winter roadsides became a fairyland, naked bush and tree clothed in ice and snow. Snowbanks lured careless drivers to entrapment.

By late November my patient appeared to have a beach ball beneath her apron. Our suspicions were confirmed by two definite and different heartbeats ticked out by the Doppler I pressed against her abdomen to magnify its noises. Velma was exuberant at the prospect of twins. David waited impatiently for the birthing.

"It's a hospital birth this time," I insisted. "We'll not risk a baby for the lack of modern facilities."

The Wengers chose Ephrata Community Hospital located at the hub of Mennonite country. The distance from the Wenger home to the hospital was too inconvenient for David to attend the prenatal classes required for privileged admission to the delivery room. Velma said he moped like a sick kitten when he learned that he could not see the twins birthed.

Hospital rules must be obeyed, but to a husband present at six uneventful births the statute seemed illogical and unfair. Husbands were allowed to stay in the labor rooms with their wives until time to move to the delivery room. I could only smile, shrug and insist that laws are made for the good of someone but I was not sure whom.

January had weeks of unrelenting freezing temperatures. Where the sun melted snow on patches of earth and road, night and shadow snatched them back to glib ice.

Velma was a balloon with fence post legs, hustling about her work as usual. It may have been the overloaded basket of wet wash, or the clumsy package she carried beneath her apron that caused her to slip on an ice patch as she stepped from the cellar door. She fell forward fracturing her left kneecap.

Near due date the Ephrata orthopedist put Velma's injured limb in a straight full-length leg cast until he could operate after the twins' birth. She struggled several days between bed and chair, losing patience, hunting for the good side of her enforced immobility. Finally, labor began.

Velma's face flushed with anticipation. Between panting contractions she smiled and chatted with David, dressed in Sunday white shirt, black bow tie and black pants under the loose cover gowns required for the labor and delivery suite. His lean close-shaven face showed only furrowed concern for his wife as he fed her ice chips, comforted and guided her through contractions. When she changed position, he lifted and pillowed the awkward cast that weighted her leg.

"Is there no way I can go into the delivery room?" David pleaded. The black hair he brushed from his face was salted with white streaks.

"Can't do it," I said. "Rules are rules."

From the Wenger's labor room I could see traffic passing on the concrete strip of the old highway to Reading. Below, at the rear of the hospital lawn, horse-driving Mennonites had built a small stable for the convenience of visiting members. They cleaned and maintained it. I chuckled, wondering how many modern hospitals could claim a stable and hitching rail.

As I waited with Velma, the evening light cast a cold glow on snow patches from last week's blizzard. The sun descended in a blast of orange along the horizon.

Delivery was not far away. The delivery of twins both excited and concerned me. David repillowed Velma's cast, bemoaning the rule about to deprive him of the delivery room. Velma panted with her pressing babies. It was my move.

I spoke to nurse Lucy Burkholder. "Velma's cast looks more like a barn timber than a leg. How will the two of us manage that thing in the delivery room? We'll be busy enough with Velma and the babies. Even moving the patient at this time of labor will not be easy."

Lucy laughed and rolled the sterile instrument table into the labor room while I scrubbed for delivery. Even David's mask could not hide a victorious grin. Velma's eyes were moist with happiness and the final stages of labor.

While David supported the cast, covered by sterile drapes, the first Wenger boy came with the ease of a pin falling through a water pipe.

Before I could finish with him and reach for a leg to bring down the second baby, its head descended into the mother's pelvis. Six minutes after the first baby a second boy lay on the bed. Two vigorous babies lay in heated cribs. No rules had been violated.

"Ike and Mike," I said, examining a placenta that appeared to be the one of identical twins.

Velma laughed and lifted her head to watch the nurse snap wristbands on her sons. "Oh no, Mahlon and Galen." She laughed. "You know, breaking my knee wasn't all bad. David got to be with me and see the babies born."

6

Visitors And Thoughts

M y hospital room contained more plants and flowers than a florist shop. When Pete returned from a week's business trip to Phoenix, he measured forty-two feet of floral gifts. People stopped by the room to admire them. Lying motionless in bed with a room full of greenery and blooms, the world seemed unreal. Surely I would awaken from this nightmare.

Word of my accident spread rapidly among my patients. Within days they began coming to admire my flowers and gaze over my bedrail. If an Amish family had a hospitalized friend or family member, I rated a visit. I recognized most of them but could not always put name and face together.

One evening a white-haired, stooped Amish woman limped to my bedside. I struggled to identify my spindly guest but did not recognize the shrunken face. "You'll have to tell me who you are. I'm afraid I don't recognize you," I said.

She pushed rimless glasses up the ridge of her peaked nose, creased a broad smile. "Oh, you never met me. I'm Priscilla Zook. I heard about you and wanted to see what you looked like." Bony fingers caressed a pink rose bud. "What beautiful flowers. So many." She spent several minutes in my flower shop before returning to her husband's bedside down the hall.

Amish woman, Lydia Glick, and her daughter Mary from Gordonville RD#1 were also strangers. "But you know my brother Amos and his wife Emma along the Strasburg Pike near Vintage," Lydia explained, laying their black bonnets on a chair. She smoothed gray-streaked black hair from a dumpling face, leaned over the bedrail and explained how Mary had slipped in the barn and fallen down a hayshoot when fifteen, injuring her neck. "Doctor said she hurt her spinal nerve."

Mary smiled, resting against the foot of my bed. She showed me her contracted index fingers. They moved stiffly when she opened her hand.

"We thought," Lydia took a deep breath and hesitated. "We thought, if it isn't too much trouble, maybe you could give us some advice." She looked at her daughter.

I wondered what I was to tell this pleasant woman, towering above me in Sunday black dress and apron. Of course. Mary must have a menstrual problem, I guessed to myself. I waited.

"Mary's been goin' with the young folks six years now," Lydia continued, shifting from one foot to the other. "She'll be twenty-one come January. She wants to marry this November. Problem is, she has trouble with her bladder. Can't always control it. Not bad if she goes often. Just sometimes she forgets herself. She can work good." Lydia exhaled a slow deep breath. Her brown eyes, fixed to my face, did not blink. "What do you think?"

Mary's shocking-pink cape, apron and dress added a rosy glow to her full cheeks. She was as still as a manikin. Black eyes traveled my splinted arms and hands. She waited.

Above all else I valued family. What would my past have been like without husband and children? I could not imagine the void. Life without the cares or gratifications of babies and adolescents. No husband to share goals and adversities.

I thought of patient Peggy Woods, confined to a wheelchair since eighteen. Three times I had seen her uneventfully through pregnancies and the delivery room. Should Mary's hopes be splattered on my hospital floor because of incontinence?

Slowly, as if pondering the answer, I smiled. "No," I said. "I see no reason why Mary should not marry and have a family."

"Thank you," Mary said. Her grim countenance changed to a grin.

She released a long breath. "Thank you."

Before they left, each woman opened a homesewn tapestry bag and brought out a gift. Mary's was a small pillow covered with a bright blue and green washcloth. Lydia laid a blue and white striped towel and a cake of Camay soap on the bed.

Gideon Petersheim's older daughter Susie came to visit. "Last winter I was driving home with a young horse from New Holland in the open wagon. A piece of white plastic rattled on the roadbank, then the wind picked it up and whirled it around the horse's head. He bolted and ran into the ditch. I bounced out and hit my head on a rock." Susie lifted both hands toward me so that I could see that the index and middle fingers on both hands were partially flexed. She could straighten them only by using the opposite hand. "I work three days a week cleaning houses in New Holland." She leaned forward, squinting through rimless glasses as if inspecting me for flaws, awaiting the answer for a question she had not asked. "The fingers don't stop me, but I wondered if something could be done."

I suggested she exercise them and consult her doctor. When we finished chatting about family and neighbors, she encased her thin face with a black bonnet and left a can of crushed pineapple on the bedside table.

Tall lanky Simon Riehl and his short dumpy wife stopped to see me when Sara's sister was a patient on the maternity wing. I had delivered four babies at home for Sara, but they were half-grown now and I had not heard of Simon and Sara for several years. Simon unhooked his coat and laid it with his big black hat on a chair with Sara's shawl before walking to my bed, leaning heavily on a brown cane.

He stroked his shaggy brown beard. "I had to give up farmin' and go to buildin' furniture." He leaned toward me, waved both hands to demonstrate fingers stiff and slow moving. "Slipped on wet grass playin' badminton. Hurt my neck the doctor said. I'm better now than at first but not sure of my feet sometimes." He waved the cane. "This is better than lying in bed. Bet you'll walk out of here too."

Before they went down the hall to visit neighbor John King and all the other Amish patients, Sara spread open the brown plastic handles of a voluminous green bag made of upholstery fabric and withdrew a square of white tissue paper, "Here, I'll open it for you."

She unwrapped the neat bundle, smiled. "Made these pot holders
for you. Put 'em away until you can use 'em." She laid the two pink
and blue flowered squares on the bed.

Another afternoon Meriam Miller visited. She hung her small
black bonnet over a chair and settled her spare frame into it, bringing
me up-to-date on the last fifteen years of family life. Her brown eyes
were beacons in a sharply chiseled face. "We've been living in South
America, then Texas," Meriam said, thin lips smiling. "We're living
near Five Points now, still tending market stands." She removed a
pillow case from a tote bag. I watched slim brown fingers deftly
embroider red roses along its edge. The white organdy Amish cap
that I had known years ago was now a smaller Mennonite one. "All
the children are gone from home but Benny." She raised her gray
head from the needlework, picked a stray red thread from the green
cape that matched dress and apron. "We won't forget the day he was
born, will we?"

"No." I laughed out loud, remembering. That day had begun with
the usual breakfast rush. I had pushed daughter Elsa off to school,
dressed a son for play in the November sunshine. The baby was
diapered when the housekeeper arrived and the phone rang.

"Can you come take me to the hospital?" Meriam asked, "Better
hurry."

It was time for her to deliver, but I transported patients to the
hospital only in emergency situations. "Where's your husband?" I
asked.

"John's not home."

Peculiar I thought, but she sounded desperate for help. "I'll leave
now."

The Miller farm rode the margin of Lancaster City with Lancaster
County along the Old Philadelphia Pike. The Miller barn leaned
south, its unpainted siding weathered gray and eroded. The empty
corn cribs were as bleak as the brown fallow fields, wild with tangled
grass and stalks of last season's goldenrod. Next year a housing
development, bedrooms for workers at RCA, High Steel or Skee
Craft Boat Works, would erase all marks of the farm.

Meriam met me at the kettlehouse door, a black cardboard suitcase
in one hand, her shawl over the other arm. "We'd better get going. I
thought John would never get off to market. If he'd known I was in

labor, he'd have stayed home. No use for that." She locked the door and lumbered to my station wagon, pausing during a contraction. "I felt like pushing with that one. Let's hurry. Wait till John gets home and finds out what I pulled on him." The slamming car door sliced her chuckle.

I laughed now, remembering the wild ride to the hospital, headlights on, horn blaring at every cross street and red light as we tore through them. Another scare but no baby in the station wagon that time.

Twenty years later Meriam still enjoyed recalling the day. Then she admired my rows of chrysanthemums, daisies and planters, laid a new towel and washcloth on the bedside table. Before leaving she leaned over the bedrail, patted my cheek, bent over and kissed it. The grief and sympathy in her face and the kiss by a patient was unexpected. It was a hot searing arrow piercing my facade.

As Grandmother lay in her casket, family and friends had leaned into it and kissed her paper-cold cheek. Immobile between rails, the room full of flowers, the kiss, the pity in the faces of visitors hurt more than the spasms in my legs. I felt like a corpse laid out for viewing.

***

The second hospital Sunday I fell apart. My head throbbed with forty drums pounding off-beat rhythms behind my eyes. The chief of the obstetrical department was in the room. "What will you do with your practice?" he asked.

"Dick, if you can find anybody to cover it, go ahead." The loss of an active practice is a loss to a hospital. "I can't talk about it today. I feel like a dice shaking in a cup. Can't anyone give me something?" I thrashed my head over the pillow. For the first time in my life I felt out of control. In my practice, nothing had unnerved me. I could talk about the weather, tobacco prices or naming the new baby while furiously fighting a maternal hemorrhage, but I could not stop the jarring in my head. It frightened me. Where had discipline and fortitude gone?

My friend left. A crowd of visitors waited in the hall, a sea of faces looking into the room. No one. I could not cope with one more guest or decision. When Pete called from Arizona, I could not speak with him. The room would not stand still. A **NO VISITORS** sign gave me the rest I needed.

Dick understood. Until a new physician came to take my practice in July, his obstetrical group generously covered my office and delivered the hospital cases. They saved a valuable practice and removed my major concern. I could focus on recovery.

Each step in recovery led to the next one. "Let's see if you can sit by yourself," Joe said several weeks after therapy began. He pulled me to the edge of the bed, then upright, my feet dangling over the mattress.

I clenched my teeth, determined not to fall over. Across the court of the U-shaped building stood the wing of the original hospital, utilized now for offices and maintenance. I had walked its halls as an intern, birthed our first baby there one steamy August. Now with breathless concentration, my eyes gripped its old bricks, white window frames and did not move.

"Breathe," Joe commanded, holding his arms out to catch me if I fell.

I sat without support several minutes. It was wonderful. "How was that?" I asked, happy with achievement.

Joe laid me down, shrugged his shoulders, half-smiled as he pulled up the sheet. He laughed. "Okay for today."

Gradually strength and mobility improved. One day as Joe exercised my legs, I felt a sudden tug and pull on my left shoulder. "Did my arm fall off the bed?" I asked.

Joe nodded. "Pick it up. Put it back on the bed."

I concentrated, tried. Too soon. My only arm motion was from the shoulder. Several weeks later when I became able to bend my elbows, Joe and Cynthia, from independent living, devised a feeding apparatus that clamped to the back of a chair. Its joints and springs fastened to my right arm with velcro. More velcro secured a fork in my hand.

"Let's see you feed yourself," Cynthia said.

Joe cut a toasted cheese sandwich into small pieces. "How could she miss that mouth?" He grinned.

The springs held my arms half-flexed and away from my body. Flapping like a crow, I rolled my shoulder forward, bent the elbow, then dive-bombed the plate to spear a bite. Often I missed the target, or the food dropped before it reached my mouth. I never ordered peas or gravy for lunch. The contraption made eating hard work. It was easier to have a nurse feed me. Besides, I would be fully recovered soon and not need the hassle.

Joe pushed and insisted. He gave much time and energy to my recovery. I tried to please him. Every noon he came to harness me into the feeding machine and tease me about the hospital fare. "How can you eat that? It's garbage can special. It's from last week's trays."

The kitchen made a special effort to send attractive food for my general diet, but we laughed at his descriptions. He was sure it was wormy or from the cattle sheds at the auction barns along the railroad.

I became more adept at spearing toasted cheese sandwiches. After the first day, I never ordered jello again. The cubes slithered away from the fork, fractured a few inches from the plate or avalanched strawberry down the front of my blouse.

Liquids, through a straw, were an easy trip to the mouth. The catheter I wore allowed luxurious amounts of fluid. After the accident I developed an intolerance to cold drinks and salt. The crab cakes I formerly enjoyed in the cafeteria burned my mouth with their salt.

When the nurses fed me breakfast and supper, I enjoyed not having to bounce my arm or spear my food to eat. Joe supervised at noon. "Be sure to eat enough. Build your strength." The longer I knew him the more he became like a mother hen.

When Joe began stopping to chat, evenings after playing basketball, I felt special. Joe had helped to organize the physiotherapy department and was its head therapist. He directed aides, secretaries, porters and kept records. He knew most of the medical staff. Having held offices and headed committees, I was hungry for news and savored every juicy detail of gossip from kitchen to surgery. He slouched into an armchair and relaxed, propped his sneakers on a stool, knowing our conversation was safe with me.

I listened to burn treatments, complaints about patients and physicians. I learned to know Joe's family and his problems. He made me feel like a whole person, like the one I had been, not a plastic manikin wheeled from bed to gym. We laughed at anecdotes, chewed over the same words week after week. I looked forward to his visits and worked harder to please him. My reward was a half-smile, half-a-compliment.

From Joe I learned that most of my recovery would occur the first year. I was not to be discouraged by plateaus in progress. "You must retrain in one year what a baby learns in several," he said. "After a year your progress will be slower." A year! In a year I would be back in practice, therapy finished.

Therapy, nursing care, naps, visitors kept the days busy. Nights. Bedtime drew the bare walls around me like a purse string. By dim lights the rows of flowers cast spectral shapes and ragged shadows on the walls. Nurses made swishing noises as they hurried down empty halls. The nurses mumbled at the desk. Bedpans rattled in the utility room. The aroma of fresh coffee drifted in from the kitchen.

Nights. In solitude my thoughts turned inward. Why did I have to lose one useless year from my life? When could I return to my office? What good could come from my tragedy? I needed someone to blame for the accident, but no one had thrown me against the edge of the bunk or wrapped the electric cord around my ankle. I had been alone. There was no one to blame, no one to sue for liability, no scapegoat. Frustration brewed and boiled until tears wet the pillow. I believed the nurses did not suspect a doctor would resort to tears until months later when I read their notes in my chart.

So many unknowns and I wanted answers. I looked forward to a discussion with my pastor. I mentally dialogued with him. As a trained counselor he would know what to say, ease the pain.

He came at the end of the first week, sat beside my bed in a black business suit, leaning against the bedrail. Initial greetings, congregational news, then a pause. "I'm a quad," I wailed. I had not even thought the word, now I spoke it. First tears burned my cheeks. Finally I could tell someone how bruised I felt inside and discuss the real me behind the false front I tried to maintain.

The pastor reached for a tissue to wipe away what I had saved for him. He had not understood. "No, no. The nurses can do that," I said. The moment had passed. Maintaining his Sunday pulpit face, he rendered a short prayer and left. Comfort and acceptance were still months in the future. I resolved to save tears for bedtime.

Nighttime thoughts searched for solid ground to moor my sanity. There must be some unseen purpose in the loss of a year. Everything seemed black. I was in the bottom of the darkest valley between steep cliffs. No way out for one used to walking the mountain tops.

Snatches of hymns played through my head. I extracted favorite phrases to repeat and dwell on. Scraps of psalms came to support me. The liturgy of morning church service, choir anthems all offered comfort in the dismal dark. I began to realize my parents' greatest gift was not the college education they had sacrificed to provide. I had always valued it for the happiness and for the comfortable life it gave me, but now in this time of enormous need the gift I drew out and depended upon was the one labeled Religious Background and Teaching.

Sleep and dreams. In dreams I again jogged my evening route through New Holland Machine Company grounds. Cold air whipped tears onto my cheeks. I felt the exhilarating thrust of the earth under my feet, the surge of blood to my head as I labored for breath. Our yellow dog ran with me, chasing a cloud of screeching killdeer from the grass between rows of red farm machinery that cast spectral shadows in the night lights.

Summer returned for a week in October. Nights were sultry. Air conditioning had been turned off until next year. It was too hot to cover with even a sheet. The window and door were open to catch any puff of air.

At bedtime the nurse gave me Talwin to relieve pain and spasms, to induce rest. I had used it successfully with my patients and asked for the shot each bedtime. One hot night before sleep came, I was aware of slowly rising off the bed, rising higher than the ceiling. Below, my body still lay propped on its left side, lower leg straight, the upper one flexed over it. Pillows wedged my back as the evening nurse had left them. The blue flowers on my gown stood out like ink blots. Slowly, I rose higher but was not aware of passing through the ceiling. I saw clearly my limp body, brown hair, the splinted arms and legs. Was I dead? Why? I had not been critical. Panic. Fear. I wanted to get down. Fighting a strong upward surge of energy like powerful magnetic rays, I willed my spirit back into my body.

The experience lasted only seconds, but it convinced me that I did not want to die as I often believed. The fear that I might leave my body again lingered. I was afraid that next time I would not get back. Details remain as clear as if it happened last night. I never again asked for bedtime medication.

As I lay in bed like a corpse, connected to bottles by a network of incoming and outflowing tubes, injected regularly with syringes of medication, it was easy to reflect how far medicine had come in twenty-eight years of practice.

During my 1950-1951 internship at Community Hospital only the A building had existed. Dressed in heavy gowns, standing for hours holding retractors during steamy July and August, had been a muggy job. Nurses patched and repatched the rubber gloves worn in obstetrics and surgery. Disposable supplies had not been introduced. Nurses cleansed, sterilized, reused IV tubing, syringes, gloves and surgical drapes. I shivered, thinking of the risks. It had required constant care to keep supplies in usable condition.

Groups of women traveled regularly from farm and village to repair or sew new doctor gowns and drapes. The hospital sewing room with its rows of sewing machines was supervised by a woman who directed the work of brown-bagging volunteers. Sometimes when passing the room, I recognized a group of Amish women and stopped to chat.

The idea of reusing a syringe or IV tubing, the risks and possibilities for contamination, the transfer of infection from patient to patient was unthinkable in present medicine. I had used only disposable equipment for years. However, when I began practice in 1951, I had a special stone to sharpen and remove the barbs from reusable needles and syringes before placing them into rubber-capped stainless tubes, 5cc and 10cc sizes. I sterilized them in my small autoclave and carried them to house calls. Individual dosage vials required a tiny saw to score the neck before breaking them open. It was embarrassing for a patient to see my occasional bloody fingers, even when using a gauze pad to snap vial necks.

Having moved into the big farm house in New Holland, Pete and I settled down to worry about meeting our $70.40 a month mortgage and paying the bill to remodel three front rooms into an office for me. Using time payments at Van Sciver's in the former umbrella factory at West King and Mulberry Streets in Lancaster, we bought the maple waiting room furniture sold at our sale when we left New Holland thirty years later. I stocked my dispensing shelves with medications, pill envelopes and boxes, ointment tins and bottles on credit from pharmaceutical salesmen anxious to open new accounts. There had been a multitude of salesmen who called every two to four weeks with new untested combinations of medications.

I placed notices of my September office opening in the local papers and with apprehension began my vigil, hoping that rumors at the hospital predicting that a woman doctor in the country would not be successful were untrue. Would anyone walk into my waiting room? Would they like me, be satisfied with my treatment, return? What would the first brave patients report to their friends? Would I fail? What if no one came?

Canasta was popular. Evening after evening Pete and I played cards in our bare kitchen at an old table given to us by his mother. I did not use appointments or have an office nurse. It was a great evening if the office bell rang three times to announce patients. Walking through the empty cubicle planned for living room furniture when we could afford it, I would leave our game and enter the office. Were my pounding footsteps hollow promises?

In December, with great joy, I scheduled my first obstetrical case. The practice was still not a sure success, but it was promising. In a year I was too busy for card games.

Many first patients were those who had already visited all other doctors in the community and were incurable hypochondriacs, but I welcomed anyone who entered my front door.

Thirty-five years after opening my practice my husband gave me a journal he had kept intermittently from July 1, 1951 until June 1961. After ten years I was no longer a young wife beginning housekeeping and a practice. By then we were halfway through our mortgage, had enlarged our house and had three children at the dinner table.

Included with Pete's journal were letters written by patients during the early years. The most prolific correspondent was unmarried Annie Burkholder. Annie was a short shy woman, pale, wispy, mousy. She wore the net cap, apron and dress of a conservative Mennonite group. Her black Chevrolet sedan, ten years old, was seldom driven further than Lancaster or more than forty miles per hour. In my office she timidly complained of chronic back pain but preferred to pour out and mail her weekly thoughts on tablet paper. She was determined to make me the perfect doctor by combining my efforts with those of the wonderful machine found in the office of her Lancaster chiropractor. In one letter she enclosed a clipping about Old Quaker Blood Tonic Capsules to help the blood. According to a Mrs. Martin quoted in the newspaper, "When I go without them, I break out in boils and my feet hurt . . . I advise anyone with diabetes to take these capsules, because they help the blood." In another letter Annie sent the contents of a horse liniment, Kendall's Veterinary Liniment Formula, she had used over several years and wrote, "And I think that the horse liniment that I rub on my hips makes me limp because my right heel is too high for me." Again, "I started to take one of Russel James Hyssop Tablets every day and I rub my left hip with liniment every day. I had some liniment that the Amish doctor had told me to rub on my back."

During my years in Lancaster County there were several Amish men, as well as women, who promoted themselves as healers and sold vitamins and advice for donations, thus not illegally practicing without a license. In one four-page letter Annie worried about her liniment because an aunt told her about a woman who had used the concoction. It made her bones brittle, and she broke a hip. Annie wrote, "They use this liniment for horses. The Amish doctor said if it is good for horses then it is good for the people also."

In the absence of hot water bottles many country people used corn bags and kept several on their space heater. Annie tells me how she made hers. "A bean bag is handier for me to use. I made a muslin bag about 14 inches square then filled it with soybeans. I put this bag in an old loaf cake pan and heat it in the oven. On the 8th of May I tried out the horse liniment alone. I did not use the bean bag at all and then I had to limp again." With Annie, as all patients, I listened to their home remedies and tales of visits to other healing establishments. I never criticized and learned much about my patients.

One scrawny emaciated young woman with pimply face and stringy blond hair used to spend her time in my waiting room selling vitamins. Jane supplemented her husband's income by urging everyone she met to try her marvelous formulas. I never felt threatened by her competition.

One woman who had called me to her house in false labor, wrote, "Sorry I spoiled your weekend. Here I am plugging away yet. I've been trying to help matters along by housecleaning. My forgetter is so busy again."

A Mrs. King sent a letter.

Dear Friend,

"A few lines this cloudy morning. I suppose you saw that I was there last nite. I guess you had just left, but it was my fault, we should have called, but I thought you were in the hospital all day. I didn't know if I should try to come again or not, but mother & I decided, since you have my urine it would not be necessary if you would give or send a bottle of pills [she means prenatal vitamins] to dads or send them down here. I have gained a few pounds but it has been six weeks since I was down there. I have about quit eating potatoes, bread, cake & pies etc. I have little to complain of, have the usual movements. Hope I need not come again and you will come here first, ha.

Sincerely,

Mary Ann King

The letter that amused me most was one in which a young husband begged for an exception to my rule that I would deliver no first babies at home. He complained about the high cost of food, coal and horse feed, writing, "I'm in the money saving business." It was at Amos and Mary's house several babies later that the pressure lantern flared, dimmed, flared and went out as the baby's head crowned. By the time Amos's mother finished fumbling about in the black kitchen for a flashlight, the crying newborn lay on the bed. When the lantern was refilled, we laughed, delivered the placenta and finished our work.

We were married two years, and separated during that second year by my internship, when Pete began his journal in a loose-leaf notebook. Many pages are yellow and brittle. I immerse myself in it, remembering those first ten years, loving the memories. Reading how he felt about our lives, I laugh and wonder how he weathered and endured. It is a great gift.

7

Excerpts from Pete's Journal

Dedicated to all suffering husbands who happen to love and marry a Woman Doctor—thereby joining that exclusive group of "Doctors' Husbands."

July 1, 1951

Today is, for all practical purposes, the day that Grace can open her office. [My internship was completed June 30th, but the office area was not ready. Official office opening was set for September 5th.] The past year has been a hard one for the husband. Since February 1st [the date he moved to New Holland] he has cooked his own meals and performed the menial chores—not to mention all the painting, scraping and high financing it takes to set up a practice before a single patient comes to the front door. We are expecting a maternity call. We have propped open the stairway door and placed the phone in the stairway so that it can be heard all the better. The joke of the story is that the bell is in the box on the wall which has nothing to do with where the phone is placed. Ah well! It is only the doctor's first case—so all anxiety is forgiven.

July 6, 1951

Grace was ironing and I had just tackled changing tapes on the old blinds in the office when in walks Jimmy Holler [Pete's schoolmate], Cookie [small daughter] and his expectant wife. Before I knew it I was appointed baby-sitter. Me, who never even had a baby-sitter of his own, to sit with a baby, a female one at that. Cookie was comfortable in her crib; I was chilled on the couch. However at 4 a.m. WHAM Cookie sounds off wanting Daddy and potty. By 8 a.m. Jimmy was father of a boy, I was the possessor of a pair of red eyes. For the Daddy and potty Jimmy promised me a bottle of wine. He bought the bottle, liked it, drank it and thanked me cordially for giving him the idea to buy the wine. Me—I still have red eyes.

Sept. 5, 1951

Today was the big day! The day Grace has been looking to for over nine long years, a day I've been looking forward to for about five years. The first day was a bust financially, morally or otherwise. Very few people knew that she was open for business. The ads in the paper won't be out until this coming Friday. She did have a non-paying customer; Mrs. Donahue needed a certificate of vaccination for Patty Ann. This waiting for the first paying customer is harder than the whole nine years put into a nutshell. In fact it can be most demoralizing. Funny thing, when the first one shows up you feel like slamming the door behind you and scooting out the back door.

Sept. 6, 1951

Believe it or not! A patient finally came into our trap and was deposited in the waiting room. He was a perfect stranger but had the two-fifty for the treatment of the foot. So the ice is broken, self-confidence restored in the heart and soul of the doctor. When the bell rang we weren't sure if the bell was ringing because a patient had entered or if I hadn't closed the door properly. When it rang the second time we were certain the trap was sprung and Grace was in practice.

Sept. 21, 1951

Our first night call was just about what we expected it to be, with of course a twist or two not in the manual. It seems that Friday [our police dog] was obtained to go along on night calls, but no, the lucky stiff slept while I took the dog's place. This being the first time the phone rang in the middle of the night, it sounded anything but like a phone. It dawned on us that it was ringing and we should answer it. I commenced by hunting the light switch on the far wall. Next time we'll have a night light. She commenced by groping over the floor for the phone. By next time we'll have a nightstand. I had better luck—hers was miserable. In fact she gave up and just hung out of bed and said, "How do you work this darn thing?" After awhile the dawn swept into our brains; we did take care of things in a professional manner. Got a complete description of what road to take, where to turn; all of which we missed when we looked for it. The patient proved to be on Bulltown Road, one of those Amish farms set off away from the road in a little dip so that it cannot be seen by the users of the road. With the moon shining and the stars twinkling in this warm fall air, the house was really beautiful. The shadows hid all the faults and the moonshine brought out all the highlights. On the hill I could hear cows grazing. This Amishman was of the old stock, no shoes and a beard, with no gas powered engines to defile his property. I believe that I could have spent the night there, just sitting under one of the trees and watching the slow and quiet movements of that which surrounded me.

Sept. 1951

One of the worst stomach turning feelings I've had is just sitting here across from Grace and doing nothing but watching and listening for that bell to go. I guess there are a number of ways you can kill this time between patients. One is to get your husband to play "cutthroat canasta." Another is to sneak into the waiting room and read the magazines that should be read by the patients, or to write a letter home telling them that you are doing better than expected, not to worry over you. It does help to bolster your morale a little too. But there is nothing that will rid you of that feeling in the stomach unless a patient walks in.

Now I guess Grace and I have played cards for two to three hours at a stretch with not the sound of that bell. By nine we would both be just playing and trying to juggle the "patient per day" average of two so that it would cover the blank evening and also give us the excuse for a brighter tomorrow. Believe me, those nights are the pathetic ones in our young life. You'd like to go to bed by nine as soon as hours are over, but you wait around until ten so that they will see the sign [electric on the lawn] and perhaps remember to come in the next day. In fact, you don't care if they come during hours or not—just as long as they come in.

Oct. 1, 1951

Today is the big day for Grace's step into New Holland's society. She was off to a covered dish supper and a chance to meet some of the private citizens in this town. Things don't always go as planned. In fact she had two patients come by 6:15 and I had to rush her back just as they were starting to eat. I couldn't tell who drooled more, her or Friday. It is now 8:25 and she has had naught but a bowl of peaches and a bowl of milk. I know she is starved. I guess the doctor's husband will get clipped for his last buck and take his ever-loving wife out to the local hamburger stand for her supper.

This chalks up her biggest day for her. She should have at least seven paying patients so it will do much to alleviate the flopping of the stomach.

Tis funny, last week her stomach flopped, growled and rolled because of no patients. This week it is because of too many patients.

The buggy rail has been put up. In fact, after a buggy parked itself in our garage it seemed that a rail was needed imminently. I spent a miserable Saturday outside digging the post holes, etc. In fact, the winds almost froze a few parts from my anatomy. One of the most fascinating pastimes a young doctor can have while waiting for patients is to play the averages. The hard part is to figure out and convince your wife that she has reached the average for the day by adding to lean days, patients who have presented themselves on fat ones. Brother, with Grace it takes some doing!

Dec. 1951

. . . take the gent, a quiet individual, it seemed, who came in with a bad back. When asked to take off his clothes to the waist he must have slipped his waist down to near his ankles. He compromised and settled for at least his shorts on.

Jan. 1952

I guess one of the things that will vex a husband more than

anything is to have a cold supper, or no supper at all. So the guy on my number one hate list is an egotistical servant of the Machine Company who cannot go to a doctor during hours. In fact, it can only be done to suit his convenience. "He" likes to have his supper on time and if he gets to the doctor by 5:45 he can be at his dinner table by 6:15. Consequently, on the nights he comes for his treatment we don't eat. In fact it is 8:30 and the poor kid hasn't had her supper yet. Just because of this one pompous so-and-so. So we could refuse him, but who is turning down four bucks at this time of the game? Heh!

Feb. 1952

I think one of the things that will always gripe me is that patient called a "Dead Beat." Of course doctors are supposed to be tolerant, but you can't live on that. Worse than that are the "Dead Beats" that tell you they only pay their bills once a month — but forget to tell you which one of the twelve. Other offensive "Dead Beats" don't pay, make more than I do [Pete worked in the office of New Holland Machine Co.] and then come for everything under the sun. Not once a day but twice or thrice is nothing unusual. But pay — what a laugh.

April 1952

Honestly, if all doctors are as my good wife, I just pity the other side of the team. Here we are, rolling along nicely, not coining it at a rapid clip, but neither are we losing out, and I think that is all breezy, when she gets a day with only one patient. So there she is, nose down, spirit down, starting to save money again by making me dig a ditch for the new water main. When just last week she was out spending it as fast as she was making it. I guess it is like all doctors. Money in their pockets sure burns like ethyl chloride on the skin. When she has it she spends it, when she doesn't have it she saves the stuff. Her latest hiding place is a daily calendar where she accumulated fifty dollars toward a new washer for Xmas. She was fooled though. The washer burned out and she had to produce the fifty dollars way ahead of time much to her embarrassment.

April 1952

Lately a maternity has been giving us a few sleepless hours. It's a house delivery and up to now the apple has refused to fall, but threatened twice. I tried to go to bed again. Sam Sagner was just coming home from work. I called him in and we both just sat around and chinned. By then it was almost four and the night was shot for both of us. Mrs. Fisher? She didn't deliver after three hours. She decided to do the wash and hang it up.

May 1952

Much has been said about the Amishman and his beard. He came in one day with a few cracked ribs. The moment of payoff came when in a moment of curiosity he looked down just as she was about to tape a strip rather high up. Temptation was great and it was all she could do to stop from laughing. But she kindly refrained from taping the beard to his chest.

Aug. 20, 1952

One of the first requirements of a doctor's husband is just like that of a doctor's wife—be ready for anything. Personnel Manager called me to give blood, said patient was in dire straights. Grace told me it was her patient, just to replace what was given.

Nov. 1952

Being a doctor's husband has taught me more tolerance toward my wife than I ever imagined I would have. Our waking hours revolve about her and only her. Best laid plans by us are changed by a phone call, something I am or was not used to. For me it was not uncommon to plan ahead three or four weeks, know what I would be doing at a certain hour on a certain day. Not now—a maternity is the most unpredictable event in the way of life. The birth makes liars out of experts, and so we confine ourselves to New Holland and vicinity.

Getting back to a tolerant husband, at heart I try to be, but sometimes, when I come home and find this scattered here, the mail all over, and shoes and stockings all over the bedroom I have to blow my top.

Nov. 1952

There are times when I'm sure Grace must have a feeling of complete helplessness. She never will say, but I can see it on her when she comes home after something has gone wrong. Usually after a birth she comes head up, chest out, swinging her bag, pets the dog, etc. But the opposite shows when all goes completely wrong, even when it is hopeless. She is depressed in spirit, listless, and the old vitality is out of her eyes. Recently two cases — a six months premature where the aid of the hospital, doctors and drugs could not bring the baby to breathe. The other — to a farm where an acetylene torch exploded, throwing splinters through a man's head. If things are low I slack off also. It takes only a case of two like these to really make you realize how small and helpless man is when the hand of the reaper claims his soul.

Mar. 1953

The urge to kill was never greater. It was a cold night, storming, visibility zero and it was 2:30 a.m. We had been at friends in Lancaster for the evening, were just ready to eat when the call came. The main road was bad enough but the dirt lane of a mile was murder and bumpy. Only with luck we didn't get stuck. Grace had to carry her light and gear from the drive to the house. Brother, what did she find, everyone in bed. Forgot about the doctor coming, plus no pain at all.

Mar. & April 1953

Grace is pregnant! We were sure of it some time ago, but having hysterics. She is having considerable nausea, and I never saw a doctor who could take care of herself. Putting up a front to the patients has been a very hard thing also. Many a time she would beat a path to the bathroom as the patient left the front door. On house calls she would stop the car to disgorge, then go on her merry way. Of course it is going to help her in her practice. The maternity cases will get more sympathetic help from now on.

Late Summer 1953

Hiding that expanding belly was quite a problem, but she gradually discarded each garment for a looser one. One night she tried on a loose-fitting dress, black, and darned if she didn't look like a street walker on Arch and Race [Philadelphia]. Gradually it became known that she was pregnant and the clientele reacted very favorably towards it.

A most fitting climax was presented to this 9 months rage when Grace delivered somewhat in a hurry and the 14 mile dash to the hospital proved to be a necessity. A baby girl, 8 lbs. of crying dynamite [Aug. 31st]. She will and has changed our habits a great deal. No longer do we pick up and leave. Her patients have reacted very nicely. I hope they will come back to her when she starts again September 8th.

[There are no further entries until January 1961, after which the entries are mostly about blizzards, obstetrical deliveries and conflicts or interruptions of care of the three children.]

Chosen at random:
Our Amish friends keep amazing us. Grace was out on calls when one called wanting to know how his wife was. I didn't know so I told him to call back in 1/2 hour or so. His answer was, "Well, I guess I don't have to know."

Thursday night Grace left for the hospital right after hours; didn't get back until 7:30 a.m. It was a night for the rascals [children] to act up. They had been to a basketball game and just a little excited. So naturally Elsa had to go to the bathroom, and also had some bad dreams. Keith had a nosebleed about 5:30 a.m. and needed comforting. Poor kid, he was so upset that his sheet had blood on it. And Lorelei, every time the others stirred, she woke up. In fact, when Keith woke up at 5:30 a.m. she took it as a sign to get up and was put out that I insisted on her going back to sleep. She wanted no part of it.

Time after time the phone rings for the ambulance to go to the Welsh Mountains to take a girl to the hospital. All sorts of reasons are given as to why she can't go by regular car — too sick, no car available, no gas for the car, etc. All the reasons Grace has to turn down. It's rough. They're nasty, call her names, etc. One accused her of wanting the mother-to-be delivered like an animal in a stable. The fact is, that no matter how impossible it is for the girl to get to the hospital, she always manages very nicely and in plenty of time.

Started to teach Keith how to tie shoelaces; what a job; I didn't get far. He is still all boy. He was dressed for Bible School when I noticed a wet spot on his pants. He had his water pistol filled in his pocket, only it leaked. He owes me 39 cents for the pistol. It is going to be a riot getting the 39 cents out of him. He claims he doesn't have a 39 cent piece and that is that.

8

Amanda's Death

During my fifteen years of general practice, births challenged me the most; each small miracle a future to be molded by choices. It was death that I disliked most.

"Hello. This is Abram S. Stoltzfus near Paradise. Can you hurry over?" the husky voice panted over the telephone. "It's my wife Amanda. Can't get her air right. We think she's dying, won't let us call an ambulance."

Bed was comfort. I wanted to roll over, pull the quilt above my ears and pretend the phone had not rung. Deep in sleep after an early night birthing with a woman in Vogansville, another house call seemed a punishment for choosing to be a country doctor.

"Right away," I answered, groping the phone into its cradle. Careful not to disturb my snoring husband, I grabbed clothes from the rocking chair beside the bed, thinking of Amanda's long fight with cancer. Her death would be the first one in a home since I began practice, and it would leave a jagged hole in my life. The past three months a bond had developed between us as we chatted in her homey kitchen, often rich with the odor of drying apple snitz, sliced apples or fresh chocolate cake cooling on her drainboard.

Often as I wrapped Amanda's fleshy arm to check her blood pressure, she spoke of past generations—how her shriveled great-grandmother rocked beside the kitchen range after supper and smoked her pipe, knocking ashes into the coal scuttle. I never saw an Amish woman smoke and was surprised to hear that any Amish woman ever smoked.

While I counted Amanda's pills and capsules, she told of her great-grandfather's story about the first Stoltzfus cousins distant enough in kinship that they could marry. Amanda acknowledged that Abram was her second cousin.

Thinking of Amanda, I plunged my feet into scuffed brown boots and hoped I could drive to Paradise in time to ease her last hours if she needed me.

The night smelled of freshly plowed fields and spring's dankness of new growth. It was as obsidian as the bottom of my black bag. I eased the station wagon onto Main Street and drove south on roads that followed fence line and cow path. My headlights shone on roadbanks wild with new grass and old brambles. Holsteins grazed pastures white with dew. Cottontails dove into bushes, and cats scrambled from warming their paws on the macadam.

Amanda's face, thin and weary from weeks of pain and cancer, occupied my thoughts. I mourned her, worried about proper bedside manner. Hospital deaths in their clinical situation had an impersonal businesslike atmosphere. Could I maintain a professional stance and emotional isolation? Delivering babies at home were joyous occasions but a home death — I was uneasy about this first death outside the hospital.

The roads were empty. The first light was the searchlight on Beacon Hill near the sleeping village of Intercourse. The signal swiveled its powerful beam, helping to guide airplanes across country by a network of such beacons.

Newport Road seemed the most pock-marked, narrow, twisted road in our end of Lancaster County. The red reflector and dim taillights of a carriage shone ahead. I passed three Amish market wagons, gray-canvased matchboxes on wheels, thumping pothole and blacktop. I imagined the joggle and jar felt by the passengers. As if whipped, the lathered horses clopped south surrounded in their own mist.

Where were these carriages rushing, 3:30 a.m., midweek? Amish farmers rarely traveled the road so close to milking time. Herdsmen should be lighting lanterns to begin feeding cows. What emergency had aroused folks?

One brown horse or vibrating wagon was indistinguishable from another to me. But the Amish often recognized neighbor and family by their carriages.

I remembered the story Amanda told on herself. Driving home from a quilting bee at a sister's home, she could not understand why her horse jerked its head with a peculiar twist. She climbed from the wagon, inspected bridle and harness for broken straps, found nothing wrong and drove home. When Abram unharnessed the horse, he asked Amanda why she had driven brother-in-law Henry King's mare home instead of their Bud. A young nephew had hitched horses to the wagons after the quilting. Henry's mare had a habit of throwing her head, especially when headed away from home. Poor Amanda was teased at every family gathering. When Amanda told me about it, I laughed and bragged that my ignition key fit only my own gray station wagon.

Maneuvering curves and cavities, I remembered how Amanda had found a small lump in her breast last summer but did not tell anyone because Naomi, the last daughter at home, planned a November wedding. Wedding season was too busy a time to think of hospitals and surgery. By December the cancer had metastasized beyond cure.

As I drove, I imagined that Amanda would lie in her back bedroom when I arrived, green window shades pulled to the windowsills. She would rest in her old mahogany, high headboard bed where she birthed fourteen children and had spent most of the past several weeks. Abram and several children would gather around her. I steeled myself to be the professional efficient doctor they expected.

Abram Stoltzfus lived along a long lane that ran between two hardtopped roads. Large farms with rambling brick houses hunkered over each end. Abram's unmarried daughters, Lizzie and Mary, lived in a small frame house at mid-lane. They earned a living sewing summer straw hats for Amish men and boys.

When Abram and Amanda retired, son Joel moved onto one farm. Abram cut off an acre and built a small white frame house along the lane. Like most Amish homes it had the traditional two front doors, a

glassed sunporch along the side and at the back door a kettlehouse
for washday and storage. Amanda continued gardening and canning. Evenings Amanda said she could rock on the front porch and
listen to the corn grow in the field across the lane. When needed, she
grannied for daughters at their birthing times. In winter she quilted
for a tourist shop in Bird-in-Hand. Abram made wooden toy animals
and lawn ornaments in his shop. He rarely missed a day's work at
the weekly cattle auction in Vintage.

Joel's home was dark except for a pale light in a kitchen window as
I entered the gravel lane. Four weeks ago I had spent half a night
talking cows and tobacco growing with Joel, while Salome labored
with her fourth baby.

It had been the first birth at Joel's house that Amanda had not
grannied for us. She usually bustled about, sorting out the proper
baby clothes, hunting old rags or fanning Salome with a folded
newspaper on hot summer nights. I had missed her constant smile,
her large shadow playing along the wall and over my work as she
waited to receive the newborn in warm blankets and dress the latest
grandchild.

I slowed to a crawl behind a carriage, its iron-clad wheels crunch-
ing lane gravel, lights off to save the battery. The horse pulled to
Abram's hitching rail beside a small barn and shop. Three tethered
bays stomped their feet and whinnied as the new arrival took the last
rail space. I parked before the white barn.

Clutching my bag, I hurried up the narrow walk toward the
kettlehouse, family entrance of many Amish homes. A bobbing
flashlight searched the dark from the enclosed porch.

"This way. Mom's in the kitchen. Use this door," daughter Annie
from Black Horse Road called in a hushed voice. She shone light on
the concrete steps.

I would rather have returned home, but followed the silhouette
into the sunporch and wondered if the shadows made her plumper
than usual or if I would soon add her name to my maternity list.

Windows and doors between the kitchen and porch had been
removed to heat the glassed room. By light from the Coleman
lantern above the kitchen table, I could see Amanda's hopes for
another season growing in plum box seedlings. There were Camp-
bell's Tomato Soup cans of cabbage, marigold and tomato plants

lining the shelves under the porch windows.

Amanda's labored breathing filled the kitchen. In terminal heart failure, she sat on the green studio couch propped by bolsters and rose-embroidered cushions from parlor chairs. She pulled each wheezed breath in waves that heaved her large bosom with gasping exertion. When she saw me, her half-open eyes lit faintly with recognition. Fluid-logged lungs were unrelieved by her rattling cough.

"Doctor—don't make me—go to the hospital—please," Amanda panted through blue lips. "I wanta—die here—with the family." Her body, thin from cancer, had doubled its size with retained fluid since my last visit.

I accepted a kitchen chair and pulled it to her couch, warmed the stethoscope in my palm a moment before laying it against her clammy chest. Soggy lung rales, air bursting through moisture, rattled in my ears.

"You would be more comfortable in the hospital. Oxygen would ease your breathing," I said.

"No—please," Amanda choked. She coughed, sucking air through dry parted lips. Her eyes were puffy, her face bloated, ironing out the usual sagging jowls and wrinkles.

"How long has she been this bad?" I asked Abram.

"The girls have been taking turns staying with us overnight for several weeks, but this began yesterday. Much worse since this noon." He dropped his unhappy gaze. "We gave in to her, but the girls thought we oughta call you now."

Dressed in Sunday black broadfalls, vest and coat, Abram had eyes that were dark sad circles. He scarcely looked away from Amanda. Standing beside his wife's death bed, Abram wore a lined face, haggard above an untrimmed wiry beard that mingled white with red in the lamplight. Gray hair, cut to ear-lobe length, ringed a nearly bald head. What Abram lost in height, he compensated for in girth. He cleared his throat and stepped into the shadows, allowed me to take his place.

Abram continued, "Said she wanted the Lord to take her from her home, with family near." Craggy lines and hollow cheeks showed the strain of sleepless nights and worried days.

"No ambulance—no hospital," Amanda gasped. Black-ringed

eyes searched the room. "Sylvia—Isaac—Benuel—Naomi—not here yet?"

Salome rubbed her mother-in-law's wrists. Sarah fanned her mother violently with a newspaper folded in quarters. They lifted tree-trunk legs onto the couch. "Let her here if that's what she wants," they agreed.

"Let her be," Abram said. He looked toward the kitchen table for confirmation.

On benches and chairs around the linoleum-covered table a ring of black-coated sons and sons-in-law hunched quietly or murmured in Pennsylvania Dutch. They nodded glum agreement. From an iron hook above the table, the Coleman lantern with its milkglass globe hissed a monotone dirge adding heat to the stuffy room. Even at night, the polished birch cupboards reflected Amanda's meticulous care. The brown pebbled linoleum shone streaks of light. A coal snapped in the stove, splitting the rhythm of the mantle clock like an off-beat cymbal.

"Good-bye children—Abram," Amanda panted, closing her eyes.

Amanda's strident breathing dominated the room until a carriage ground stones on the lane and a stubby, black-shawled woman rushed through the kettlehouse doorway, breaking the room's tension.

Sylvia smiled recognition to her solemn brothers at the table. Amanda's struggling breaths sobered her chubby face. She kissed her mother's cheek, "Hello, Mam." She shook Abram's hand. "Glad I got here in time," she whispered. Tears wet her eyes as she turned to take bonnet and shawl into the parlor. She shook hands with everyone before relieving Sarah at the fanning.

"Good-bye," Amanda repeated, gave a deep gasp and stopped breathing.

Clock and lantern intruded like a gong in the silent room. I caught Amanda's last irregular heartbeats in my stethoscope. I nodded to Abram. The months of waiting for cancer to claim its victim were over. Our grief lay in the void of Amanda's struggle for breath. Lizzie and Mary began to remove pillows from the couch and lay their mother flat.

"No, no." Abram stepped forward, arm outstretched. "No. I want the other children to see her like she died," he commanded. "They will be here soon. I want them to see her sitting up, like she passed away. God is good. We wouldn't wish her back again. The way she suffered these last days—." He lifted silver-rimmed glasses and wiped his eyes, blew loudly into a white handkerchief.

The funeral director would remove Amanda's body long enough for embalmment, then return it, clothed in a white dress and lying in a plain, pine-box coffin. I had been to Amish homes after a death. The coffin would sit on trestles in the parlor, all furniture and carpet removed.

Flowers never embellish Amish funerals or decorate their cemeteries. Stark floor boards would add solemnity to the cold room, its green window shades pulled to polished pine sills during the two or three days of vigil before the funeral. Black-clad Amish neighbors and *freundschaft* (kinfolk) would come to embrace and shake hands with the grieving family, offer condolences, food and assistance at the funeral. After services a serpentine procession of chalk-numbered carriages would drive to the graveyard, then return to Joel's larger house for a meal.

With no telephone closer than a non-Amish neighbor two miles away or the pay phone at Paradise, my promise to telephone Mr. Brown, the funeral director at Christiana, and ask him to come for Amanda was an opportunity for the family to keep Amanda until the remaining children arrived. It would be forty-five minutes before I reached home and the telephone.

Abram's family spoke in whispers, grateful that Amanda had not been forced to go to the hospital, that her death had not been postponed by medical intervention. The men were glum. The women shed silent tears into white handkerchiefs, spoke of their mother's freedom from this life and from the pain of cancer suffered the past sleepless weeks.

Sorrow was contagious. I looked at Amanda, scarcely realizing that a friend was gone. My pleasant routine visits were finished. Should I have insisted on hospitalization? But why, when cancer consumed her? I could have done nothing more for her.

It was still the black of early morning when I packed my bag and shook hands around the room, took a last look at Amanda surrounded by pillows and loving grief. I started through the sunporch,

Annie beside me. I tugged her sleeve gently and whispered, "Do your people usually keep their dead in the position in which they die?"

She shook her head. "No," she murmered. "It's just because Dad wants it that way."

"Oh yes," Abram called to me. "You'll be passing preacher Elmer Zooks on the way home. His wife Mina is sister to Amanda. Could you stop and tell them? There's no close neighbor with a phone. Thank you."

Two carriages waited on the hard road to enter the lane as I drove out. A third still hurried south several miles away near Elmer's lane. I drove between whitewashed board fences beside grassy ditches and parked along the Zook's wire yard fence. In the dark I stumbled up the irregular flagstone walk under a leafing grape arbor. Spidery vines interlaced overhead in rambling roadmap designs and cast erratic webbed shadows at my feet.

Elmer's house and its inhabitants were familiar. Flu, measles and farm accidents had taken me to their home. I remembered the day Elmer amputated the end of two fingers in a V-belt. On postpartum leave from the office, I had driven him to the hospital.

I had frequently aroused Mina at night from her back bedroom to travel with me as granny for a daughter in labor. This morning, knocks on the sunporch door accomplished no more than shudders along its flimsy wooden wall and trembles in the glass panes. The porch and kitchen doors were unlocked. I groped around table and chairs hoping none stood out of place waiting for my shins. Heat from the range guided me around the stove toward the bedroom.

"Anybody home?" I called. "It's Doctor Kaiser. Anybody home? I hate to get you up." Did Elmer keep a loaded gun for intruders? I wished I had not been so quick to agree to stop here.

Grunts and grumbles beyond the door. "Who's there? What's wrong? Old Harry get out on the road again?" Elmer shouted, remembering the night I led his driving horse off the road and knocked on the bedroom window to wake him. Elmer appeared barefooted in the sleeping room doorway, silhouetted by a dim kerosene lamp on the bedside stand. He pulled suspendered broadfall pants over an unbleached muslin nightshirt, rubbed squinting eyes with the back of a broad calloused hand.

"Somebody having a baby?" Mina called, sitting in a pile of quilts. "I don't know who it'd be." She straightened her muslin nightcap and pulled a blue flannel gown to her neck.

"No. It's Amanda. She died this morning," I answered.

"Well, Mom. You know what must be done. We'll go over right away," Elmer said. "A blessing for Amanda that she could go. Abram will need us."

Pondering my first home death, I drove home slowly. I was not sure what I had expected. Life and death had assumed new aspects. Amanda's family had not wailed or complained. Death for them seemed an extension of life. Lines of Bryant's poem *Thanatopsis* came to me like a hymn.

> *So live, that when thy summons comes to join*
> *The innumerable caravan which moves*
> *To that mysterious realm, where each shall take*
> *His chamber in the silent halls of death,*
> *Thou go not, like the quarry-slave at night,*
> *Scourged to his dungeon, but, sustained and soothed*
> *By an unfaltering trust . . .*

9

Your Baby or Mine

There are myths and fears about babies being mixed up in hospital nurseries, but I never thought it could happen to me, happen at a home delivery. One minute you hold your baby in your arms, the next moment someone else sees it as theirs.

Stevie Smucker called from his neighbor's telephone at 3:30 a.m., "Can you come now? It's Sallie's fifth you know."

I hated to slide out of warm sheets into a cold night. I tired of balancing cooking, babies and husband with patients and office hours. Too often blind justice tipped the scales away from family. In fantasy I quit practice many times, but I was entangled in a web of commitment, monthly lists of women who expected me to come when they called. Our relationships, repeated year after year, nourished me. I was an addict who did not want to recognize my affliction.

Winter nights husbands hated to leave warm houses for more than one telephone call so they often waited until the last minute. Sometimes they waited too long. Groping for clothes laid out on a chair at bedtime, I telephoned my office nurse, five houses down Main Street. "Anna, I'll pick you up in ten minutes."

"Ten minutes bed to street," I often bragged to Pete. Before running from the bedroom, I nudged my husband awake. He shook his pile of covers like a spaniel after a swim. "The Smuckers live at Mount Tabor, three miles south of New Holland," I said. "I'll be back in time to nurse the baby."

"You'd better be." Pete rolled over without missing a snoring beat.

He was right. At five months Lorelei slept all night, but she indisputably believed that milk came exclusively from breasts, never a hard rubber nipple. I expected her to sleep until seven before waking, hungry and screaming if not fed. I hated to disturb her, take her with me as I had always done my newborns, carrying black bag in one hand and a baby on the other arm. My infants had slept in nurses' lounges, on Amish couches or on spare beds. Returning before Lorelei's breakfast time seemed a safe gamble.

Stevie had reminded me, "Remember how fast Sallie was the last time? You didn't get your coat off before the baby came."

I hurried down our hall, not worried about Elsa, age seven, or Keith the kindergartner. Pete could get them breakfast and off to school. I looked at the baby, not even squirming in sleep.

The stars were out. Frost crunched under our boots as Anna and I went up Smucker's concrete walk and through their cold kettlehouse into the kitchen heated by a monstrous brown space heater crackling with fresh coal. Heat felt good. The stale odor of last night's supper mingled with that of cow stable, clinging to a row of shoes beneath the stove. Anna hung her red coat with my corduroy on hooks behind the stove with a row of black garb. We went into the adjoining bedroom to see Sallie.

She lay on a bed prepared according to printed instructions. On top of a clean sheet she had laid a square of protective plastic, then a cloth-covered newspaper pad. Her bed and dresser were a matching waterfall pattern, popular several decades ago.

"Guess I have everything you need," Sallie said, motioning toward a gray enamel washbasin, a pile of clean white rags and neat stacks of baby clothes on the bureau.

I crossed the flowered tan linoleum, opened my bag and laid out a box of plastic gloves and a sterile instrument pack on a bedside chair. "You won't be as fast this time," I said, after the examination.

"Then I might as well get up and work," Sallie said. "Maybe it'll help move things along. It would be good to have this baby before the kids get up." She slid a blue seersucker housecoat over the ragged nightgown worn for her birthing. She fumbled under the bed for tattered gray slippers.

"The milk truck gets here 'bout eight o'clock. Guess I'll go to the barn, get an early start on feedin' and milkin' case you want me later," Stevie said. His voice became demanding. "I sure wanta be in here when Sallie needs me. Be sure to come call me or set a kerosene lamp in the kitchen window if things get serious." His tone changed to doubtful. "Remember, I can't leave a milker on a cow and run. Gotta give me plentya time. I'll watch for a light."

He sat in his pine swivel chair at the head of the blue linoleum-covered kitchen table and laced up ankle-high work shoes cracked by mud and muck. A worn and dusty old coat taken from behind the stove had seen many hours in the barn. His blacktop hat wore ragged stain margins along its band.

In a culture of similar names, repeated like a stutter, the Amish are fond of nicknames. It was no wonder that Stevie was known in the community as Shorty Smucker. Dressed in wide-brimmed hat and bulky coat, he would have looked more like a smiling, half-grown adolescent, not a father of four and master of his farm, if it had not been for his bushy black beard. He was as round as a tree stump. His short arms ended in hands like soup plates. Ruddy cheeks were set in a face as round as the full moon, his nose a pointy afterthought. Boyish brown eyes and Amish ear-lobe length, bowl-cut hair with bangs might cause a stranger to ask him if his father was at home.

Satisfied that his wife was not alone, Stevie went down the walk to the barn, swinging a pressure lantern in each hand. I daydreamed, imagined him hurrying into the stable, closing the door quickly to keep the body heat of the cows from escaping into the crisp night. The cows would stretch out their black and white Holstein necks to lick up every last grain of feed, rough tongues scraping the concrete trough like sandpaper. Neck chains would rattle, cows yet unfed bawling with impatience. Their sweet breaths would mingle with the dust and odor of fresh-forked hay and warm milk streaming into buckets from the pumping milkers. Quiet would settle over the herd as loaded udders were drained. I reminisced the barn of my youth, thought of my own breasts soon in need of emptying and searched my dress for telltale wet circles.

While we waited for Sallie's labor to progress, Anna sat on the

kitchen couch beside the closed sewing machine. I took a chair near
the hissing Coleman lantern hung from a hook above the table. We
talked winter weather, babies and cooking with Sallie while she
swept the leaf-figured linoleum with a broom, then stacked last
evening's supper dishes, a mishmash of size and pattern, into brown
cupboards. The lantern cast a honey glow onto the cream-painted
walls and varnished cupboards, worn smooth along the edges of
doors by the busy hands of housewives.

During contractions Sallie stopped working to hold her abdomen.
I could tell by her even panting that birthing was not imminent.
Occasionally she drew more snugly the ends of an unbleached
muslin kerchief covering her light brown hair, combed tightly from
brow to bun at the nape of her neck. Shuffling around the room, she
turned the baby blankets warming on a clothes rack at the stove,
glanced at the mantle clock metering time behind the kitchen table.
Five-thirty. The ticking beat out time toward seven.

At home Lorelei would soon be stirring for breakfast. I could feel
the need for her in my breasts and remembered the painful mastitis
and 104° fever I had suffered when Keith was a baby. I had been
gone from him too long while waiting with Alta Sensenig in the
hospital labor room. Then I had scrubbed for her delivery before
going home to my own baby.

"Guess I'm not so fast this time," Sallie said. An apologetic smile
crossed her oval face. "Sorry to keep you waiting so long."

We heard a cough and huffing in the barn as Stevie started the
diesel engine to begin milking. The kitchen's green window shades
were pulled to the deep varnished sills, in case a neighbor might see
lights and guess that Sallie's birthing was in the wind. I raised a
shade. Outside all was dark except for boxes of light marking the
stable windows and larger distorted blocks reflecting onto the gravel
lane. I stood at the window wishing the night to stand still or Sallie to
deliver within minutes. Neither was likely.

If I went home, my patient's anxiety would probably speed up her
labor, and she would deliver without my help. If I did not go home,
Lorelei would soon be a squalling hungry baby and Pete an angry
frustrated husband.

Anna drove my red station wagon back to Main Street and returned a half hour later with clean diapers and Lorelei in her car bed,

a collapsible affair that rested on the rear seat and hooked over the back of the front seat. The baby slept until I lifted her from the bed.

Sallie was concerned about her family too. Soon her children would awaken and want to come downstairs where they were not wanted during their mother's labor and delivery. Amish children are not included in birthing events.

While I changed my baby across my spread knees, then nursed her, Sallie began breakfast. She brought from the pantry an enormous box of saltines, butter in a small crock, a basket of eggs and an iron frying pan. She carried a pail of milk in from the cold kettle-house.

"Can you eat some eggs for breakfast?" Sallie lit the black propane gas stove under a pan of milk. Her deft thin fingers cracked eggs into a bowl without breaking a golden yolk. The odor and sputter of frying eggs spread through the kitchen. She filled soup plates with saltines.

I sat by the window burping my blanket-swathed baby against a shoulder. The sun's first light separated night from day along the horizon. As the minutes passed grotesque shapes took form; Smucker's grape arbor, the plastic-wrapped martin house on its pole, the skeletal windmill rising like an airport tower above the well in the yard.

The stable lanterns went out. Stevie's bundled apparition sauntered between the gateposts and started up the walk. Suddenly, as if stung by a bee, his silhouette ran for the kettlehouse door.

We heard his boots stomp the cement floor in pounding steps. He tore through the doorway into the kitchen like a summer gale. He could not see Sallie pouring hot milk over butter-dolloped crackers. She slid eggs over the saltines, two lidless orbs in each dish.

"Why? Why didn't you call me?" Stevie panted, throwing his coat over a chair, hat on top. His face was red, eyes flashing anger. The thick beard did not hide his indignation. He looked like a policeman catching a man at a crime.

Stepping farther into the kitchen, he saw Sallie as she started toward the table, a dish in each hand. He saw her still large protuberance hanging like over-ripe fruit, then Lorelei bobbing against my shoulder, and he began to laugh. Stevie aimed a long stretch of Pennsylvania Dutch, his native tongue, at his wife. She grasped her pendulous pear, spatula in hand, and joined the hilarity.

Confessing that all the Dutch I needed to know were *esse* and *gelt*—that "eat" and "money" would carry me through any requirements—I rediapered my baby and wondered at their secret.

"Stevie saw you at the window holding your baby and was upset because he thought it was our baby," Sallie finally explained. "He thought I had a baby, and you didn't call him in. He sure wants to be here when ours is born."

Sallie set three plates of breakfast on the white cotton tablecloth. I have never eaten at an Amish table without a tablecloth, even if it was stained or perforated with holes from hard use. Stevie, Anna and I bowed our heads for silent grace, ate our stewed crackers and finished with sweet crumbly shoofly pie washed down with coffee. Before we rose, another silent grace ended the meal. Sallie, not permitted breakfast until after she delivered, walked around the kitchen wishing that her baby would come soon.

Laughter must have helped. Her labor intensified, fortunately, because the children upstairs had dressed and were impatient to come down. They became louder and more boisterous. Stevie took a box of crackers, a handful of pretzels and slices of cheese up to them to satisfy their hunger and keep them occupied.

At seven Sallie went to bed. Several contractions later a wailing baby lay on the sheet. Anna covered the newborn with warm blankets, then carried her off to weigh and dress her while I delivered the placenta. Stevie hacked a hole in the half-frozen garden to bury the placenta from the dogs and the children.

The chattering children came down the stairway, nine-year-old Mary toting soggy Aarie on one hip. Melvin, seven, and Amos, four, slid along the wall behind Mary. Silence captured them when they spied Anna and me. They were even more astonished to see my baby in her car bed.

Sallie gave directions. "Melvin can go to school. I'll keep Mary home to tend Aarie and fetch things for me. That's the advantage of goin' to Amish school. The teacher will understand. My mom lives near Quarryville. Stevie and Mary can manage until we send a driver down for her."

Lorelei had gone to sleep. Her stomach satisfied, the rest of the world was of no concern to her. I picked up *MY* baby and went home.

10
Rehabilitation Center

This was the day. I did not want it, had not ordered it, but it had arrived. I had reluctantly agreed. This was the day to leave the friendly care of the hospital that had been a part of my life since the first day of internship and go for rehabilitation among strangers. I chose City Rehabilitation Center near Reading because it was closest to New Holland, about thirty-five miles away.

Joe had been the first to warn me. "They think you should enter a regular rehabilitation center," he said.

"Who's they, and why?" I asked. After seven weeks I could walk through the gym if a therapist held the back of my slacks for balance. Every evening I sat in a chair a few minutes longer to increase the time out of bed until my body ached to lie down. I fed myself lunch each day, fork fastened to my hand with velcro, the arm supported by springs. My swollen hands were useless; I carried a Foley catheter and its bag everywhere. A newborn had more mobility and as much dependence on others.

"You'll get special care and retraining," Joe said. "They have a large warm swimming pool as well as a psychiatrist. Most patients like you go through depression."

Joe received a turned-up nose, two inches of my tongue and a laugh. "I won't need a psychiatrist," I vowed. No one in my family had ever had an emotional problem. "That's a joke."

The "they" were the physician head of physiotherapy and my friend the neurosurgeon, whose name headed my chart and orders. The neurosurgeon was kind, generous and thoughtful. At his next visit he confirmed Joe's statements. "They'll get rid of your catheter at the rehab center. Urinary tract infections can be a problem in spinal cord patients," he said, smiling. "I remember a case during my residency. The man kept his catheter inside his hatband. He built up a resistance to any bacteria it carried." The doctor grinned, shook his head, remembering.

I imagined the man in a restroom unwinding his red rubber catheter from inside his hatband. Ingenious.

"You'll do fine at the rehabilitation center," the neurosurgeon continued. "We'll send you by ambulance."

On moving day the New Holland ambulance waited at the emergency room exit. A screaming ambulance chills me. The hair on my arms stands out straight, despite the times I gratefully watched one drive down a farm lane. My request to ride by car to the rehabilitation center was lost in the scuffle of "doing what was best."

There is nothing wonderful about an ambulance trip, even when anticipated. The atmosphere of this ride was calmer than the one seven weeks previous when admission for quadriplegia cut the night air with anxiety.

Wrapped in sheets and blankets, arms buckled straight to the body, a patient's view from a rolling litter is restricted to monotonous ceiling tiles passing overhead in hypnotizing repetitious squares. The gurney wheels corners, thrusts and bumps into elevators. Attendants mutter polite but unimportant phrases like "here we go," or "almost there, keep your elbows in."

The stretcher slips into an ambulance like a letter through a slot. The overhead view is white ceiling. The odor is hospital. The ride is a hybrid mating of dump truck and an Amish carriage. An open radio crackles messages to the county emergency units. Through side windows the world passes in the blur of a fast forward movie.

In seven weeks the snappy fall days of October had changed to cold December. A soft drizzle closed in the day and curtained the east coast from the sun. Leaves, once red and gold, clung to the ground in brown patches and soggy wads under naked maples and elms.

A chill air carried rain and the odor of moldering summer. It cooled my cheeks as I was unloaded at the brick rehabilitation hospital. Tied and wrapped I seemed more like a delivery of beef to the kitchen. The thought was both funny and depressing.

More acoustical tiles, reeling corners, the smell of disinfectants, the rattle of pills at the nurses' station. Pete signed admission papers. A "one, two, three," count slid me onto a bed, sheeted taut as an ironing board cover.

I said good-bye to my friends of the ambulance crew and lifted my head to view the large room. "Wrong room," I whispered. "There are men in those two beds."

"No," Pete said. "We were afraid if you knew this was a mixed ward you wouldn't come."

A nurse smiled and pulled the sheet to my shoulders. "Two men and two women. New experiment. You're all quads."

Right. I could not have imagined nor would I have consented to sharing a room with men. Gripped without choice in the jagged teeth of a decision made by some unknown authority, I decided to be open-minded and give it a try. One thing for certain, no hanky-panky possible with four quads.

Large institutional windows brightened the room. Jimmy's bed was beside the window. Mike's across from mine near the door. Cindy also had a window bed. In the aisle shared by Jimmy and Cindy a life-sized teddy bear straddled a commode chair. One of my pet peeves was the gift of stuffed animals to adult hospitalized patients, sending the message that for some reason their brain had also become disabled. Mine was the only bed not surrounded by greeting cards, stuffed animals or medical paraphernalia.

Mike and I were foot-to-foot across an aisle. "A big wave knocked me down at Atlantic City last July," Mike told me later. "When my wife didn't see my bald head come out of the water, she hunted around and dragged me to the beach. Thought I'd drown before she found me. Had an operation for a broken neck before I came here, in another hospital."

Mike was short, bony and mid-fifties. Nature had covered his skeleton with the barest necessity of skin and flesh, giving his face the phantasmal gaunt appearance of a man in the shadows. His smiles were pleasant but fleeting. Uncontrolled tremors, like aspen leaves quivering in a breeze, shook his feet. Depressed about being a quadriplegic and losing his ability to manage the family electrical business, he was quiet and polite. His wife visited every evening, his grown children several nights each week. Conversations were short except when he argued sporting heroes and baseball scores with Jimmy.

Jimmy had become adept at turning his *Popular Mechanics* and baseball magazines with a mouth stick, pecking page over page. Watching with repugnant awe, I shuddered wondering if I would be expected to use one. I had only heard of the rod used by quads to draw pen-and-ink designs on greeting cards. Jimmy clamped the top of the T-shaped stick between his lips and teeth directing the free end like a pencil.

"I should'na dived off that dock," Jimmy said. He laughed, dimpling smooth cheeks, "That old bay got me. Too shallow. I laid on the bottom 'til I thought I'd die. Couldn't figure what had happened to me. My cousin came in and pulled me out." Barely twenty, brown-eyed Jimmy was a mixture of youthful sunshine and moments of black clouds. His many friends visited several nights each week or took him out barhopping and to ball games by wheelchair. I tried to imagine him drinking beer through a straw. Or, did his pals lift his glass for each swallow? Jimmy's parents anticipated his eventual discharge by remodeling their house for wheelchair access, adding a room and special shower. They accepted their son's need for dependent care the rest of his life.

"How do we transfer you?" the nurse asked me at admission. "What can you do for yourself?"

"I sit unassisted, walk a few steps with help." I had been proud of my accomplishments. "My hands are swollen and useless. I can bend my right elbow enough to touch my face, move my shoulders the most." Now it sounded like so little progress. "I stand and pivot to transfer."

Stand-pivot is the toe of the patient's shoes against the nurse's toes. Knee bracing knee, the nurse lifts the patient under the arms, pivots on the balls of the feet and transfers the patient onto a bed or into a chair. It is safe as well as easy on the attendant's back.

The nurse examined the sore over my tail bone. "Have your

husband bring in a hair dryer to dry it. We'll put medication on your coccyx. Have to watch all quads and paras for sores. Between occupational and physical therapy schedules you won't have time to lie in bed."

The sore healed, but with no sensory perception below the shoulder level, I could easily burn myself with the hot packs we could request for spastic painful shoulders. My roommates were complete quads and had more skin problems than I did. Since small hemorrhages in my spinal cord had caused my injury and the cord was not severed, I knew that my full recovery was only months and intense therapy away. It had been promised.

Until rehabilitation was complete, I accepted the assigned wheelchair. "Look out behind," I called down the halls and out of elevators. My arms never became strong enough to push a wheelchair forward. Hoping unwary victims saw me in time to escape, I pushed backward with my feet, like a grasshopper in reverse.

At City Rehabilitation Center, Occupational Therapy fit a plywood lapboard, like a highchair tray, over the wheelchair arms. It helped secure me and was a way to transport things. I could also read a book or magazine from the surface.

"Will you bring me a *Woman's Day*?" I asked Pete. "And a rubber thumb like money counters use so I can turn pages." A nurse pushed the adhesive cot over my middle finger. Squeezing the magazine between the heels of both fists, I dragged it onto my lapboard. Pushing page over page, leafing recipes, I fumbled from slimming exercises to home remodeling. Cookies, pies and casseroles were not interesting without a kitchen or the ability to hold a mixing spoon. Homemaking articles and child rearing were worlds I could not relate to from a hospital. Cover to cover took an entire exhausting evening, but I accomplished it without a mouth stick. They were for the permanently disabled. My disaster was temporary.

The third day the porter pushed me to the psychiatrist for my appointment. Behind the mahogany desk a balding man in goldrimmed glasses began asking questions about my accident.

"I'm fine," I said. "Having no problem adjusting. Everything is going well. I don't think I need any help."

"Good," he said, folding small white hands across my chart. "Would you be willing to participate in the group sessions twice a week? They might benefit you."

"Yes," I agreed. I might learn how my roommates felt about their disabilities if I could relate to them in a group. What thoughts and anxieties lay unspoken behind their easy banter? If only the doctor had asked me why I felt so sure about myself, if only he had pursued deeper into my thoughts. Often I have wondered if it would have eased later adjustments.

Most evenings Pete and friends visited. One night Pete brought a jar of peanuts. I chased the capricious nuts up and down my blouse several times before getting them into my mouth but was exalted to have regained enough motion in my right hand to press a nut between thumb and first finger. I bent the elbow and lifted my shoulder. If the peanut did not fall, I could lean forward and catch it between my lips. I had conquered the world. What happy satisfaction a baby must feel as it learns to finger morsels into its mouth.

"I think I could feed myself if you taped a fork into my hand," I told a nurse as she fed me the day after admission.

Occupational Therapy brought a spoon and fork, the handles pushed into four-inch lengths of round rubber, like garden hose. My semi-clenched fingers had no grasping power. An ace bandage bound the fork into my hand. I ordered food from the menu that I could spear easily. This was happiness, one step above the springs that suspended my arms during meals at the hospital.

The first day I struggled to harpoon three forkfuls, using shoulder and elbow muscles. Concentrating on arm position brought the food to my lips. I fought to remember how to coordinate feeding. For several days three trips per meal exhausted my arm. Volunteers from the community who came at mealtime to feed patients forked the remaining carrots and potatoes into my mouth. Slowly the number of self-fed trips increased, but someone had to uncover the plate, cut meat and vegetables, wrap the fork into my hand and finish the meal when I tired.

Then a wonderful thing happened. Marty came from New Holland one noon meal each week. We were friends at church; our children shared activities there and at school. In addition to beets and beans she fed me news of shared acquaintances, church events and hometown doings. I will be forever grateful for her kindness. Her visits were as refreshing as an arctic breeze in mid-July, satisfying a thirst for home and familiar things that I had not recognized as missing.

One evening Barbara, head nurse in obstetrics at Community Hospital, carried a heavy stack of charts to my bedside. As my friend reviewed cases, I dictated progress notes, case summaries and final diagnoses. I was tying off and snipping the loose ends of my life as a physician. Only the present mattered.

"Tomorrow's shower day," a nurse announced. After seven weeks of bed baths, even the word "shower" sounded wonderful. Twice a week we were swathed in towels, seated on the ring of a bottomless shower chair. Its contrary casters each chose to roll in diverse directions. The unfortunate nurse then shoved and pulled the wrapped mummy into a tiled shower alley which connected our ward with four women in the adjoining room.

At last a shampoo. It was like rain after a long drought. Warm water and suds cascaded through my hair and over my shoulders. The nurse was only slightly splashed and barely wet-footed. I felt renewed and clean for the first time in weeks.

Alone — the first weekend at the rehabilitation center. After therapy Friday afternoon my roommates were gathered like chicks under the wings of a brood hen and taken home to their families. Evening hung over the empty beds in a dark silence that seemed to accuse me of some unnamed crime or unanswerable fault that found me too guilty to be released into the world. In the void of catheter-wielding nurses working and chatting behind drawn curtains during bedtime undressing and teeth brushing, I missed my new friends. It had been eight weeks since I had seen New Holland.

Sunday night Cindy, Jimmy and Mike returned from furlough and routine resumed. When would I be allowed home visits?

"You can go home weekends," the doctor told me several days later. "And the week between Christmas and New Year if someone in your family will learn to catheterize you every four hours."

After admission my continuous catheter had been removed and intermittent bladder catheterization instituted every four hours. "Soon you will be able to void again," the nurse told me as she removed the Foley. I had lost bladder function when I lost everything else. The little red tubes became an important part of my routine.

Home. I could not wait until Pete returned from business in Arizona. Both daughters lived in Colorado. Certainly our two sons at home were not candidates for the procedure. Pete could do it.

"No! No," Pete shouted, pacing the foot of my bed. Panic froze his round face. He blanched from stubbled chin to the Arizona tan on his bald head. "You know I've never gotten involved with any part of medicine. No, I won't do it." Skittish as a big fish in shallow water, he grabbed his coat and left.

I had forgotten how he had broken into a sweat when he crushed his finger, fainted the night my aunt fell down the steps and I stitched her torn ear as she sat at the dining room table. When the children were small, Pete had mopped their upset stomachs off furniture and rug when the job nauseated me. He had cleaned up puppy messes and changed diapers. No doctor could have wanted a better phone answering service than Pete, but he could not help in medical situations. In my self-centered world of recovery, I had remembered only my own struggles and the word "home."

Pete's "no!" wet my pillow with tears. All night I felt defeated, boxed in by insurmountable rock cliffs. Home so close, within sight, impossible. I vowed to catheterize myself every four hours. Good, but I could not grasp the stiff slippery tube between my unresponsive fingers, could never guide it into the urethral passage to the bladder. Had the story of the catheter in the hatband been a forewarning?

By morning I was tired and depressed. Ann, the seven-to-three nursing supervisor, took time from her busy day to stand at my bedside. She held my hand. "Is there anything I can do to help?"

"No," I answered. Fresh uncontrolled tears rolled across my cheeks. My hurt tumbled out in an icy avalanche of words.

"Men!" Ann was recently divorced.

In our heart-to-heart we shared views on the obstinate, egotistical, self-centered, domineering, inconsiderate male sex. I felt better.

"Maybe your husband will change his mind," Ann said, wiping my face with a tissue.

"Okay, what do I have to do?" Pete said that afternoon. Grim with resignation, he sighed, opened the sterile catheter kit, awkwardly pulled on plastic gloves and under supervision catheterized me the first time.

Home. What would it be like? Would my family be able to move me around? I felt vulnerable and afraid.

Mid-December was cold. I needed a coat but could not move my shoulders and arms backward to push the second limb into its sleeve. I was a stiff, uncoordinated, gigantic baby. We remembered an old Logan cape. The wool cloak slipped easily over spastic shoulders as stiff as curtain rods. A thick knitted hat and heavy scarf made me an overwrapped package as the front door of the hospital opened and my warm breath floated before my face in a white frosty mist.

Stand-pivot moved me onto the car seat. Out of the supportive wheelchair for the first time, I felt as unbalanced as a round-bottomed toy clown swaying side to side. Pete swung my feet into the car and tightened the seat belt. Stability returned. I was sure that I would fall over at road curves and stop signs. I pressed my shoes against the floor mat and fought to remain upright until we drove into the garage at New Holland.

I was sure that the dog would be glad to see me. Formerly my shadow, Lady circled living room chairs and hid under the dining room table. Was she afraid of the wheelchair or punishing me for deserting her? I had anticipated tongue licking and wild tail wagging. Disappointed, I waited until she decided to renew our friendship. The next Friday Pete helped me walk into the house. He brought the wheelchair in later. Lady slowly renewed our friendship.

Pete's mother, age seventy-six, had walked across our backyards every day since my accident to cook dinner for my husband and the boys. Oma prepared a good homecoming supper. Keith and Paul forked mashed potatoes, pork chop and peas into my mouth. It seemed funny, unreal. We laughed a lot.

The boys became as adept as Pete at transfers. Paul, a high school junior, chatted about his car and its problems. Keith had finished college and talked about poinsettia Christmas sales for the troop of Boy Scouts he served as leader. The big house seemed cold and drafty. I huddled like a hibernating bear beside the living room fire. Wrapped in a blanket, I watched family activity whirl around me. I felt useless and detached, a guest in the home I had managed, directed and served.

Pete unfolded the twin-size studio couches in the living room, easier than attempting the stairs. He undressed me at night, clothed me in the morning. "I'm no nurse," he said often. I waited under the covers until he built a living room fire and prepared breakfast. Accepting this dependency came because I knew that this new pattern was temporary. Independence would be restored in several months.

In two weeks the girls would be home from Denver for Christmas and routines would be easier.

Elsa had graduated from college; Lorelei was a freshman. When they arrived they made light of my dependency, bought duck-headed pins for "Mom's birdseyes" and laughed. The cutesy pins embarrassed Pete. He hated them, saw nothing funny in his wife's diapering.

Ever since the girls had attended elementary school, we had spent one pre-Christmas day shopping and eating in a restaurant. One afternoon following therapy, they came to the hospital for the annual spree. Elsa pulled a wool hat to my eyes. Lorelei scarfed and wrapped me to the ears. We sallied into Christmas.

"I can't see things down here in this wheelchair," I complained, wanting to choose items on store counters.

"How's this?" Elsa asked. She lifted a pair of men's socks from a stack. But I wanted to see everything, not only the front items on counters. I became impatient if I saw something to my right and my chair pusher steered left. Lorelei carried an assortment of flannel shirts to me because the racks were hanging too full of Christmas sweaters and jackets for my chair to pass through the narrow aisles. It was difficult to get a sales girl's attention from a wheelchair. People talked above my head. Eye contact at my level seemed an effort. I labored all evening in the agony of frustration and birthed a loathing for wheelchairs.

My daughters easily managed the stand-pivot-sit maneuver, loaded and unloaded me from the car at shopping center and restaurant. We decided on a seafood shanty.

"Stop acting silly," Lorelei cried, sprinting behind Elsa and me. "Stop! People will think we're crazy." Our joviality and the speeding wheelchair humiliated her.

Elsa ran me around the building twice, pushing and giggling, looking for the entrance. A cold wind knifed our cheeks and teared our eyes. We laughed too much.

The restaurant was crowded, its aisles barely wide enough to admit the wheelchair. The girls tugged off my wraps as I had pulled off theirs during awkward toddler years. To be fed in the hospital was acceptable but to be forked each mouthful in a restaurant, arms hanging like Raggedy Ann's, was conspicuous. I wondered how Cindy and Jimmy felt when their buddies carted them around. Between their bites, Elsa and Lorelei took turns popping a french fry or shrimp into my mouth. People stopped eating to watch.

"Take me back to the hospital," I said. Enough was enough.

Christmas season moved at a snail's pace. The holidays seemed a commercial mockery without gift buying and wrapping, baking and decorating. The tree at the nurses' station, the children who caroled the halls were as flavorless as flat ginger ale.

Each evening I watched black and white TV from a toaster-size box suspended like a dentist's drill over my bed. Most programs were Christmas specials. Rudolph, the Grinch, Perry Como, "Amahl and the Night Visitors" were a mockery, a world across a cold void I did not want to cross. I wondered if Christmas would ever be merry again, wished Christmas would go away so TV would show other programs.

"Change my channel, please," we quads frequently asked the evening nurses. "Scratch my chin. My nose itches."

The inalienable right to rub and scratch had been pirated the moment of spinal cord injury. I remembered how cows rub great trees barkless with their scouring. On television politicians and newscasters, the President, snatched a rub at ear or nose, unable to resist a polite scratch, even before the camera. In our ward, nurses scratched an itching nose or ear, rubbed an eye, changed a TV channel. The need for a good hard scratch began as an unconscious desire. Neglected, it built to a burning pain. If ignored long enough the need went away, but it took perseverance and distraction.

But Christmas did not go away. "Merry Christmas" was everywhere with tinsel, packages and the countdown of days. I remembered holidays past—annual cookie baking with the children, always the Friday after Thanksgiving. I remembered every one from the first year Elsa was old enough to spill flour on the floor and eat more raisins than decorated eyes and mouths of the gingerbread men. I smiled, recalled Christmas pines that appeared to be molting because small hands dropped the tree balls. I thought of packages scantily clad in red paper and bound with yards of Scotch tape, surprise socks or blouses too wonderful to keep secret.

I remembered Christmas Eves with slow-birthing women. Pete, Oma and the children waiting impatiently to eat our special German supper—potato salad, herring, *gehactus,* balognas, hard rolls ready for the table as soon as I drove into the garage. On frequent trips from the Amish house to my car phone I gave hope and often false promises to my hungry family who did not want Christmas food and packages without Mother. There had been no choice. Duty and obligation had stolen my time, over husband and children. Every year I anticipated a Christmas uninterrupted. Somehow we had always muddled through. Some years we were lucky and holiday babies arrived at night or early in the morning.

I remembered Christmas mornings when Pete kept the restless, tussling children in the stairway until I came home. For them it was unthinkable to rush into the living room to unload Santa's stockings before Mother returned from delivering a Christmas baby. They never waited long. I was just as anxious to begin the day's activities.

"A few more minutes. She's here now," Peter told the four. They lined up on the steps, youngest on the lowest step, the eldest highest. "Now," he called when I had thrown my coat over a chair. He poised his camera and, stepping aside, allowed the stampede to rush toward bulging stockings hung at the fireplace.

We were a half-inch from delusion and tragedy the year Santa nearly did not get to our house, the year Mary Beiler birthed a Christmas baby.

11
Christmas

Every Christmas I worried about the collision of patient and family, knew tragedy would strike eventually. I wretched at the possibility, torn jaggedly by loyalty to both.

Christmas Eve snow dropped around the station wagon like soggy feathers. It clotted against the windshield wipers, falling to the ground in long chunks, too heavy to drift. Bush and tree swayed humpbacked under their white burdens.

Pines and yews beside porches and on lawns nested gemstones of colored lights and brilliant Caribbean birds feeding on kilowatts set out by generous householders. The veil of snow along Route 23 reflected spectrumed light into the dark palm of night. It seemed I drove this routine road to Lancaster the first time.

"If Mary Beiler has her usual short labor, I will soon be home in bed," I thought, still humming "Silent Night." It had been the last hymn at Christmas Eve church service.

I had pushed baby Paul, limp as wilted lettuce, into his snowsuit and argued Lorelei into jacket and quilted pants. Elsa and Keith had tussled over the ownership of a red scarf.

Now as the big station wagon splashed through slippery slush, I reviewed our Christmas Eve. My husband's parents celebrated German style. Dessert had been Christmas cakes and cookies brought from secret places. Finally we had opened long awaited gifts.

I dimmed the headlights, slowed as a passing car splashed dirty mush over the windshield. Tomorrow the holiday would continue when my parents arrived for a roast beef dinner and more gifts. Everything was completed except four limp stockings dangling over the fireplace. Plenty of time for them after Mary had her baby. The stocking stuffings lay hidden in my closet behind shoes and skirts. Only I knew about them.

Amos Beiler had warned the answering service, "Tell Grace to come right away. I don't think she'll have to stay here long."

I took Peter and the children home from the church, called Patsy the town's phone answering service, then continued to Mary and Amos, an Amish couple halfway to Lancaster. The Christmas service still whirled through my head.

The old brick church had been lit only by fluttering candles and white bulbs on a tree hung with chrismons, Christian symbols cut from styrofoam and decorated with silver spangles. They flashed tinseled celebration into the nave. Banks of poinsettias surrounded the lectern and pulpit. Red-bowed pungent pine garlands draped the white walls. The energy of carols attacked even the weary with infectious holiday spirit.

"Merry Christmas" greetings mingled with fresh snowflakes as we tightened scarves and snuggled deeper into our coats when we left the church and met the cold midnight air.

An usher had tapped me on a shoulder. "Call your answering service. Patsy called the church trying to reach you."

I continued toward Lancaster through clinging flakes. At Bard's Crossing I turned south onto an untracked sideroad, the snow muting engine noise as I steered between fence rows and roadbanks onto a ridge. AMOS K. BEILER lettered a dented mailbox. His shadowy farm lay a long field's length below the road. Like a gap-toothed first grader, a blurry opening in the barn wall pointed out the far end of a lane, deep-furrowed on each side by soft demonic ditches. Beside the dim gloomy barn, the old brick farmhouse slept in a stand of bald and silent snow-clad maples. Spouses bedded for a long winter night.

From former visits I knew the lane was a straight line from mailbox to barn wall gate. If my car slid into the muddy gullies, it would take a team of Amos's mules to pull it out.

The station wagon eased onto the lane and slowly followed the headlights to the opening in the wall and through it. I turned the car around and headed downhill toward the road in case the weather turned worse and tried to trap me beside the barn. My car phone would pick up a signal here, but in this gully, behind the barn, calls out would be impossible.

I picked up my bag, hunted the concrete walk to the kettlehouse and stepped into Beiler's warm kitchen.

"A blessed Christmas to you," Mary greeted me.

"A blessed Christmas to you," I answered, shaking snow from my brown corduroy coat and hood. I noticed the Bible on the kitchen table lay open to the Christmas story in Luke.

"It's different tonight than with the last baby," Mary said. "Amos can be with us tonight and you're not in a family way too this time."

At her last delivery Amos had been hospitalized after mutilating his hand in the corn picker. With her husband away from home and his mother too disabled with arthritis to assist with a new baby, Mary had opted to deliver her baby in the hospital. Only two weeks from delivery myself, I had stopped at Beiler's farm to transport laboring Mary. Mommy Beiler, who lived in the nearby *Dawdy house*, had wondered which of us expected to deliver first.

"How is Amos these days?" I asked Mary, a petite woman no taller than my chin. Much of the family's managing fell on her slim shoulders — the farm bookkeeping, directing and disciplining the children and most important, discreetly allowing Amos the impression that he directed affairs.

"Amos does pretty good if he gets his rest and takes his medicine. I see to that. His nerves have been bad since the corn field accident."

"He's upstairs sleeping?" Before examining Mary in the bedroom, I warmed my hands over the square space heater between kitchen cupboards and a green couch. Coal glowed red through transparent oval windows in its door.

"Yes. We'll call him down near baby time. Things go better around here since Sammy's turned fourteen and is out of school."

"One day a week school?" I accepted the bright cushioned rocking chair Mary pulled from the unheated parlor.

"Yes. Josiah Beiler teaches Saturday school in our district for

children fourteen and past eighth grade. Have to obey the law."
Mary's thin face was grave acceptance. Moving around the kitchen
on slim quick legs, she was a chippy sparrow.

"A new baby will be a great Christmas gift," I said.

"Little Mary is two. She doesn't seem like a baby. We'll all enjoy a
new one. The children won't want to leave it to go to Christmas
church with Amos at John S. Stoltzfus's near Witmer."

"Do you expect guests today?"

"Not on first Christmas. Second Christmas, December 26, is
visiting day for our people. When folks hear in church that we have a
new baby, we'll have to put heat in the parlor stove, have plenty of
visitors."

"What will you cook for Christmas dinner?"

"We killed three chickens yesterday. Sarah will be thirteen next
month. She can stay with me and keep house two days until nurse
Annie Petersheim comes after the holiday. We'll probably keep her
from school this week to help at home."

Amish homes showed little holiday decoration in comparison to
my house, wreathed and garlanded from front to rear. An overladen
Christmas tree blinked in our living room. In Mary's kitchen
crayoned paper chains draped the wall under the mantle clock.
Three construction paper, school-made cards with "to Mom and
Dad" scrawled in uncertain letters dominated a dozen commercial
greeting cards taped to cupboard doors. Eight plump naval oranges
filled a bowl on the table.

"Mother and Dad Smucker bought a crate of oranges and gave
every child and grandchild one for Christmas, also a nice handkerchief," Mary said. She paused to breathe long and slow during a
contraction. "Mommy and Dawdy Beiler gave each one a candy cane
and a silver dollar."

"Christmas gifts are over for you?" I looked at the mantle clock on
the wall behind the table. 2:00 a.m. At five centimeters dilation Mary
could be hours from delivery or five minutes from precipitation. I
hoped for five minutes, or at least within an hour.

"The children couldn't wait for their gifts. I made Sammy a new
coat and pants for Sunday; Sylvia and Sarah, good dresses and white
Sunday aprons plus handbags; Amanda, a dress and school shoes.
Mary got a blue dress and I sewed a dress, apron and a little cap for a

new doll. We bought Christy a wooden barn with cows, horses and sheep from old Jake Beiler's shop on Brethren Church Road. They all got a new pair of stockings too."

The clock ticked the night away. 2:45 a.m. I had to get home, play Santa before going to bed.

From her lounge chair Mary continued in her quiet monotone. "We still have a Christmas dinner at Mary and Kore Smuckers near Meadville with my brothers and sisters as soon as I can travel with the baby. We'll exchange gifts with the names we drew at our picnic last summer at brother Seth Smucker's place."

By 3:15 a.m. Mary was six centimeters. Four more to go. She caught me watching the clock.

"Don't worry, I'll have this baby before milking time." She raised a green window shade and looked toward the barn. "The snow's stopped. It's good to have you here. Amos couldn't take losing sleep all night."

No need to reply. I lay on the kitchen couch and drew my coat over tired shoulders.

Mary paced the kitchen stopping to pant during contractions. "It's a good thing the Beiler Christmas dinner is over. We had it here early December. I drew Mom's name. Sister Elsie Riehl drew mine. I gave Mom canned goods for her pantry. I got sewing needles and material for a summer dress. I'll get it made soon as I'm allowed to treadle the sewing machine again after this baby."

At 5:00 a.m. Mary woke me when she called Amos downstairs. The clock clawed time slowly. The vision of empty stockings and four tearful faces stabbed my imagination in vivid apparition. I rubbed my eyes. Every year I had worried about missing Christmas.

"Looks like you had a good sleep too," Amos said, combing red beard and tousled black hair at the hand sink beside the kettlehouse door. "Time to think about the milkin'." The crow's feet disappeared from his coarse face as he squinted at the clock and reached for silver-rimmed glasses.

"Amos, Grace and I will go into the bedroom," Mary said. "You call Sammy down to do the feedin' and start milkin'." She stopped to pant. "I'll have this baby soon now."

Amos grinned a reply and shuffled stocking-footed to the stair door. I watched and tried to imagine Pete bearded, in black broadfall pants with leather suspenders.

At 5:23 a.m. Mary birthed a baby boy with scarcely more than a puffy contortion of her narrow face and the squeezing shut of her brown eyes. The placenta delivered within minutes. There were no sutures. "We already have a Christian. We might name him Joseph. The children can decide. Maybe this one should be Amos."

The husband chuckled, "We'll let you know when you come again."

A few minutes past six I stepped from the kettlehouse onto frozen snow. Quieter than the crunch under my boots, wind whispered in the maples. Silence blanketed the folded white hills along the horizon. Stars punctured the black sky. I would get home barely before my children awoke to raid Santa's stockings. If no one else had a baby today, Christmas could still be a great day.

12
After Christmas

When I returned to City Rehabilitation Center after Christmas, the idea of leaving it was barely a germ. But once nourished, it grew beyond containment. Not that the fire had anything to do with my decision.

"Fire! A fire!" Jimmy called one night. We were all asleep.

Whirling red and white lights streaked across our yellow ceiling. They reflected on the snowy pines along the rear driveway lighting them like Christmas trees. No siren, but the heavy truck idling under our windows sounded like a fire engine. It could not be an ambulance. They loaded and unloaded at the front door.

We lay in the dark like forgotten statues in a warehouse. Where were the nurses? Why didn't they come? The halls beyond our closed door were silent. Would we be pushed in our beds out into the winter night? Men's garbled staccato voices, muffled by windows and space, mingled with our fears. We sniffed for smoke. None. Why didn't someone come?

I was the only one in the room who could stand. But getting out of bed without help was impossible. Trussed hands and feet, I was helpless. My hard plastic foot splints would have hit the polished tile floor like roller skates. Newspaper stories about patients in nursing homes dying in their beds during a fire rose vividly in my imagination. Was this our end?

We waited. The sound of racing motors. The flashing lights slid over the walls and disappeared between the pines.

"A little fire in a hamper in the laundry," the night nurse reported when she opened our door. "Nothing like a little excitement."

I was happy to resume exercises after Christmas vacation. Skilled nursing care and hot showers were a luxury. The holiday at home had been good, but after a week I was an eagle in a robin's nest, pushed, pulled and fed. Most of the time I sat blanketed before the fireplace depending upon the family for action. Frustration wore claws as I watched others doing the Christmasy things that other seasons had been my responsibility and pleasure.

The phrase, "you did it enough years, now it is our turn," held no solace. The laughter, the teasing seemed contrived. My wheelchair was an ugly intrusion into our holidays. The kitchen was too small for Oma, the girls and my chair. My giving advice on a recipe or locating a utensil constituted a highlight.

Back at City Rehabilitation, I could lie on a bed not remade daily into a couch. Personal care was a business, not a game played by a family painfully aware of reversed roles. It was good to return, also to know that I was not forgotten by my community.

While at City, Lancaster's morning newspaper requested an article about my progress. It was an opportunity to communicate with Amish friends too far away to visit. Most Amish homes subscribed to the morning paper. I had heard a rumor that the Amish community was considering a collection of funds to help defray my hospital expenses. Thinking of my many patients who struggled day to week to pay their own bills, I was embarrassed, touched by their willingness to sacrifice for me. I could tell them that I had hospital insurance.

Eugene Kraybill interviewed me in the visitors' lounge. I did not want to appear disabled. Before the photographer took pictures, I carefully pulled both hands across my lap and away from the chair's arms to hide my wrist drop. Later an Amish friend said that she noticed the swollen fingers. I noticed that my hair had a plastered-down, uncombed look.

The journalist wrote that I missed delivering babies. "Happiness used to be a warm wet baby in my arms. I don't know how to do anything else but be a doctor," he quoted. True, plus home and family. While other doctors played golf, my hobby had been a vegetable garden, freezing and canning. Four children and Peter consumed any time not spent with patients. The article ended with my belief that I would be back on my feet. "And those squirming squealing babies will once again be warming the cockles of her heart."

The rooms and halls of the rehabilitation center were full of heartrending patients. Four ladies recovering from strokes occupied beds in the room next to ours. Stroke patients, often one arm in a sling, limping on a braced leg and frustrated by speech difficulties, seemed the unhappiest people. Sometimes they sobbed during therapy. Several of these patients, like Herbert, had had repeated strokes.

I met Herbert from Lancaster County in the gym. "All I want to do is get out of here and find work." He pulled the words from his mouth like taffy.

"I'll talk to my husband, see what he can do," I said.

He grimaced a crooked smile that wrinkled a sallow face, tapped his four-legged cane on the floor and laughed. "Don't forget. I'll count on it." His bald head reflected light from the long windows as he emphasized his words with a nod.

Whenever I met Herbert, we confirmed his job, but I speculated that he would be fortunate when he could drag himself from his chair to the table. "Don't forget that job," he would call across the gym, face contorted, pale eyes lit with the hope in our game. I felt lucky that my problem was not a stroke.

Leg amputees, mostly diabetics, came to the gym twice a day to practice walking on their new prostheses, as welcome to tender stumps as a hot stove to a bare hand. While I exercised or sat waiting in my wheelchair, I scanned the assortment of plastic legs, dressed in socks and shoes, scattered about the amputee practice area like spare parts in an auto store. They intrigued me, and I wondered if they felt different to their owners than my numb legs did to me. I gawked at the strapped-on limbs moving between parallel bars hour after hour until the patients seemed glad to escape their stern and persistent therapist.

Tommy was a prototype of too many of the head-injured young

men I have seen in rehabilitation centers and convalescent homes. Loose gravel had skidded his speeding motorcycle into a tree. I imagined my sons in Tommy's handsome face. What would it be like to visit Keith or Paul, unable to recognize me after years of mothering? How many decades lay ahead for this mindless son, strong of body? What cost in money, worry, time and lost possibilities? Tommy's black wavy hair had grown over his head scar, but he was a drooling, uncomprehending infant in a man's body. He grinned a lot or laughed, unless denied a wish which could send him into a raging tantrum. His slurred speech scarcely constituted conversation.

One evening as the snowbanks outside our windows turned orange and supper trays rattled along the hall, we heard a commotion among the nurses. "He's gone. Not in the hall or lounge."

Tommy had eluded the watchful nurses and escaped outside. Through our windows, we saw him tramp in the dusk, ankle-deep in snow, clad in a blue, short-sleeved shirt and gray pants. Within moments nurses caught him under the pines and returned him to his room across the hall.

Patients like Tommy strengthened more than ever my resolve to continue the *no motorcycle, no motorbike* ban we enforced on our children the day they put away their tricycles, straddled bicycles and longingly ogled Harley Davidsons.

My visitors at City were limited by the inconvenient distance from home, but one evening Henry Beiler and his father visited. A quadriplegic, Henry hooked an arm over the back of his wheelchair for stability as we talked.

Henry had been disabled for several years. One night while roughhousing with other teenage boys at a Sunday gathering of young folks, he received a karate chop to the back of his neck. Not understanding the seriousness of the paralysis caused by their horseplay, his friends dragged him home to the kitchen couch. They believed he would recover in time for morning milking.

Bearded Aaron sat beside my bed balancing his black flattop hat on a knee, reviewing news from the Amish community. Theirs was the cream of visits. Henry's younger brothers and sisters had been among my baby deliveries. At one birth Henry's mother and I were both at term. During my years of general practice, I had been the

Beiler's family physician.

Henry had rehabilitated at City Hospital after his accident and knew many nurses and therapists. It was good to see old friends, especially ones who shared a similar problem.

I was glad that my cord injury was not complete like Henry's and my recovery only months away. I was moved by Henry and Aaron's visit, knowing they had paid a driver to bring them to the hospital. How many times the family must have traveled the route when Henry was at City for retraining physiotherapy.

A physiotherapist requires four years of college. Margo, therapist for my roommates and me, had graduated several years before beginning work at City. She was as thin and shapeless as a table knife, mid-twenties and half-a-head shorter than my five-foot-eight. A wintry blast could have blown her scrawny shadow down the street and around the corner. A health faddist, Margo indulged in fasts, purges and unique diets. Blond hair either fell shoulder length around her pale bony face or, fastened with a long metal barrette, cascaded down her back. At home she kept goats and practiced yoga.

"I'm your therapist," Margo said my first day. When she smiled, I wondered if her parents had spent as much money at her orthodontist as I had for my children.

On morning and evening trips to the gym, Margo moved me from one piece of exercise equipment to another strengthening arm and leg muscles. Holding the elastic at the back of my slacks, as Joe had done, she walked me around the gym for gait training. The day she took a movie of my walking, I did not want to believe my loose-jointed hips moving up and down at each step like pistons in slow motion. I had been proud of my accomplishments before I saw the film. Would I ever walk normally, head high instead of eyes focused on the brown tiled floor, concentrating on each step?

Margo was friendly but impersonal. After working on the equipment, I lay on a table while she exercised fingers, legs, arms. Her eyes roamed the room watching other therapists work their patients.

The first weekend she accidentally took my chart home with other papers. Nurses frantically searched our room, the wheelchairs and the gym before beginning a new one.

If Margo fasted too harshly, weakness kept her home and another therapist or an assistant took her place. I resented her absence, her inability to exercise me in my urgency to rehabilitate.

We four quads were Margo's therapy responsibility. While one of us worked at a machine, she supervised another. Often we four were in the gym together. Once she forgot me as I exercised. Exhausted from a full day I dozed, struggled to stay awake, swayed on the seat and nearly fell to the floor. When the supervising physiotherapist noticed my problem, I was returned to my chair and wheeled upstairs to bed. Sleeping was easier than staying awake. Therapy was painless, but the effort left me tired and sore.

When our family dispersed after the Christmas holidays, I did not know that a pet peeve would end my stay at the hospital. If anything ticked me off, it was people who could not keep their minds on the job they were paid to do. When a check-out girl in the supermarket gabbed about Saturday night's date to her friend checking out the next line, I avoided that girl and the store. I had paid for a period of her time and courtesy as she totaled my purchases. Rude ignorance of customers irritated me. Also, the diversion could cause a mistake.

Late one afternoon, the final straw overbalanced my discontent with City. Gym activities had thinned as supper time approached. I lay on a table exercising finger strength against Margo's resisting hand when Cindy's new electric wheelchair arrived.

Margo could not resist a toy. "Excuse me a moment," she said.

I did a slow burn watching her unpack the chair, then ride around the gym laughing, gyrating, backing. When Cory the porter came to push me upstairs for supper, Margo put me in my chair, gym time over but unfinished. I felt as cheated as if a clerk had returned five dollars change instead of ten. Margo's crass insensitivity chafed me.

Another source of dissatisfaction was our ward. A room with two men and two women was tolerable, but I never became comfortable without privacy, particularly during personal care. The thin curtains sieved sounds of bedside commodes, catheterizations, doctor examinations, nightly snores and grunts. It was demeaning. As wardmates we chatted and shared but were of four varied interests and ages. We never became intimate. I had been a good sport long enough.

Cindy and Jimmy complained out loud. They wanted recreational activities, active games, dances and social interaction with other young people. Jimmy agitated to go home. Cindy planned a transfer to a special spinal cord facility.

Group psychiatry sessions, in our room twice a week after lunch, had been a failure for me. "What do you want to talk about?" the doctor had said. "Let's hear what's on your minds."

Cindy and Jimmy requested organized activities for wheelchair patients. I listened several days before revealing my greatest concern. "It's my hands. When will I be able to use them again? They don't feel right."

The doctor ambled from the center of the room to lean over the foot of my bed. "Touch your hands to your face. Do they feel warm? Then they're still a part of you." He moved away to repeat promises that organized games were being considered as an activity for young patients.

An hour's nap at noon was more valuable. After lunch the nurses pulled the curtains around my bed, and I slept until gym time.

During the last month I had become stronger, better able to feed myself without fatiguing or dropping food onto my lap. I could stand longer. My Foley catheter had been replaced by four-hour intermittent catheterization for residual urine, and I was able void on my own. Through digital stimulation, stool softeners and laxatives I had learned what to expect of bowel training. But I was still stand-pivot, could not use fingers, was unable to dress or undress, completely dependent.

I found no fault with City's nursing care, the hospital or physiotherapy. Saturday and Sunday at home were fine, but our house was empty during most of the week. I could not be alone. Also, I needed more therapy. Dissatisfaction and the idea of leaving the rehab center grew like a pinch of yeast in a batch of warm dough. I knew where to go. Community Hospital. The therapists there were as qualified and more caring. Its gym was not as fully equipped and the Hubbard tank could not compare to exercise in a heated pool, the therapy I enjoyed and regarded particularly valuable. In City's ninety degree water I felt less disabled, learned easily to walk between submerged parallel bars, retrained my legs to climb steps, strengthened arm muscles in the buoyancy of water.

Community Hospital was home, where I wanted to be.

Pete agreed. Lancaster was closer to New Holland. I phoned Joe. "I want to leave here."

Joe came to City the next evening, set me in my wheelchair and pushed me into the lounge. We planned the transfer. This time I would be admitted under the service of friend and physiatrist Doctor Richard. Joe and I discussed my requests.

First on the list was a call bell. When I arrived at City Rehabilitation Hospital, Cindy had a call bell that operated by pressing her head against it. Jimmy could call a nurse by using a mouth-operated button. "Ask Cindy or Jimmy to ring for us," the nurses had said when I asked for the same convenience.

Often my roommates were at therapy during the day when I wanted a nurse. At night both slept so soundly that it was impossible to wake them and our door was usually closed. I had to shout to bring a nurse from her desk at the far end of the corridor. Nighttime bedpans often arrived too late, frustrating me as much as the itches I could not reach to scratch. Why could I not have an adapted bell? Was I a second class patient?

"Occupational Therapy can fix one for you," Joe said.

"Is there some way I can take a shower?" This was a luxury I would miss, suds and hot water washing through and over my neck. Below my shoulder I felt nothing, but I smelled as clean as the perfumed soap, felt refreshed and invigorated.

"We can put in a hand shower and have Independent Living from Occupational Therapy give you a shower several days a week.

"Could I have my own wheelchair?" I asked. At my last admission to Community Hospital, repeated searches for a wheelchair irritated the nurses and jeopardized my schedule. At City every patient had an assigned chair beside their bed.

"Yes."

"What about going home weekends?"

"I think we can get home privileges. We'll have to talk to the hospital administrator." Going home on weekends was an important part of rehabilitation. "You will have to sign a release form every time you leave the hospital," Joe explained.

"One more important request," I said. "My back and shoulders are as stiff as a tombstone. Could Doctor Edgel give me osteopathic treatments?" They had been refused under the neurosurgeon's care but Richard understood and would probably agree. I wanted every advantage possible.

"And my hands?" I raised swollen fists.

"I have an idea to reduce the edema in your fingers," Joe said. "We'll give it a try. It will take me several days to get this schedule set up."

"I'll stay here this week, then, if possible, move to Lancaster mid-January."

Joe wheeled me back to my room and laid me on the bed. "This hospital won't be happy when they find out you want to leave."

"You can't leave," my young Korean doctor said. "You're not ready to go." She tapped my chart with her pen. "I won't discharge you."

"Then I will discharge myself," I said. "Sign myself out."

The hospital argued but I would not be dissuaded. A hospital cannot imprison a patient. I had often advised maternity patients to go home after two or three days during the years when the obstetrical department had had a mandatory five-day postpartum stay. For patients without hospital insurance, each day meant another pair of school shoes, a mortgage payment, money to help a needy neighbor. If I signed myself out instead of a doctor writing a discharge order, it released the hospital from any responsibility for the patient and gave City the right to refuse me admission in the future. My decision surprised the hospital.

"What happened? What's wrong?" the staff and nurses asked. "Did we do something?"

Evening nurse Joan took time from her charting to sit beside my bed. She rested a hand on my arm, smiled, sighed. "We're worried about you leaving us so soon." Her unhappy face and furrowed brow bore out her concern. She leaned over my bed. "Is there anything the nurses did wrong?"

"No," I answered. "Nursing care has been excellent."

"Margo?" She rose to leave.

I nodded.

"You are not the only one to feel that way. Won't you stay?"

When I could not be persuaded, the doctor signed my discharge.

"You'll be sorry. You will be back," Margo said. The nurses, the wheelchair porter, the therapist who exercised me in the pool agreed.

Were they right? Was my decision foolish? Would I return?

13

Community Hospital

Work toward recovery began in earnest when I returned to Community Hospital. My first admission to Community had been like elementary school; the weeks at the rehabilitation center, high school. Now I had reached college level.

Three months of disability had passed like a puff of breath. Progress seemed turtle-paced. By now I had expected to be running again, but I could walk only if a balancing hand gripped the back of my slacks. My hips flimflammed like a rag doll in the hands of an imaginative child. It was impossible to get up if seated, transfer myself from bed or chair, dress or undress. Someone had to take me to the bathroom, brush my teeth and cut food on my dinner plate. I longed for the first splintered ray of independence but there was none. Arm numbness persisted. From my chest down through my toes I felt only the vibration of sudden contact. Both hands were swollen and useless. I could move both wrists and the bases of the fingers. Meals were a combination of self-fed, with a fork bandaged in my hand, and nurse-fed. Three to six months remained of the time promised before I could return to office and patients. I was impatient, often depressed, but not discouraged.

All the requests I had made of Joe before returning to Community were fulfilled. Three mornings a week Joan, from Independent

Living of Occupational Therapy, swathed me in towels and pushed me, a wrapped mummy, down the hall where a hand shower had been installed for my benefit. Joan pulled a wash mitt over my hand, soaped it and I dabbed at legs, chest and abdomen. Joan finished the bath and shampooed my hair.

Occupational Therapy jerry-built an ingenious call bell. By squeezing a lever between my shoulder and the mattress, a peg pushed the button that buzzed my room number at the nurses' desk. The problem became one of guarding this prized possession from forgetful nurses who moved the contraption beyond my reach to the far side of the bed or laid it on the bedside table.

For years I had known Doctor Edgel as a fellow staff member, but now he became a friend as he manipulated and stretched my back and limbs. He was not only the most generous, caring, kind man I have ever met, but also unrelenting, brutal and determined as he administered the osteopathic treatments I had requested. He was past retirement age and practiced his profession for the love of it and out of faithful commitment to patients. His fingers were steel bars against my sore spastic areas, but he knew where to apply his art to acquire desired relaxation. Three mornings a week his lanky body bent over me. Sensitive hands, as large as dinner plates, stretched muscles and limbered vertebrae. I lay as stiff as a dead mackerel on the leather-topped treatment table. When Joe and Edgel flipped me from front to back, like a fish in a pan, I screamed with pain. Spasticity came back, but faith in the therapy and determination for improvement kept me returning. Edgel adopted me as his special project, resolved that I should benefit from his years of experience.

As Edgel spoke he had a habit of tilting his head back to see close objects through his bifocals. A clipped mustache arched his upper lip like a brush stroke. White hair framed a square face that reminded me of my handsome grandfather. Carefully enunciated words snagged his speech with remnants of years below the Mason Dixon Line.

A wheelchair of my own. How had Joe managed that when they were a premium possession on every floor? I guarded it. A special water-filled cushion to sit on was a great idea to relieve pressure on my buttocks, but I felt unstable, pitching from one side to the other like a ship about to be swamped in a storm, sure I would land on the floor.

With wheels, the entire hospital was mine. Weak arms could not move a wheelchair forward. I pushed backward with both feet, calling, "Watch out, here I come," as the chair bumped through the swinging doors that separated departments. If they swung only one way, I waited for the next person coming along to open them for me. Until my arms strengthened, elevator buttons were difficult to reach. Everyone was in danger as my wheelchair backed zigzag through doorways, out of elevators and down halls. I visited former patients on every floor, shared their family and friends, enjoyed ice cream and cake parties brought in by visitors. I became a confidant to decisions and problems.

Among my convalescent cards and letters Harvey wrote about his wife's hospital fee of the previous fall. Martha had delivered a baby on the 24-hour plan. Harvey's letter was a taste of practice days. I had pursued so many patient bills that I often imagined the doughy woman in billing hiding behind her filing cabinets as I came through the doorway. When I backed into the office, she smiled, remembering past encounters, ran a fleshy finger down Harvey's itemized bill, checking each item. The $12.50 overcharge correction would be as important as $100 to Harvey. It felt warm and good.

Each day after lunch, an hour in Occupational Therapy strengthened arms and hands. Using cardboard knitting mill cones, piling cone on cone, I broke through restraining barriers of tight weak muscles, until finally, before discharge, I could reach no higher. To strengthen wrist muscles I rested my arm on a 4 × 4 block of polished wood, attempting to hold my floppy heavy hand out straight. After several weeks I was able to extend it five minutes, then longer.

One day after a stroke patient had cooked a practice meal in Occupational Therapy's kitchen, I asked if I could stand at the sink to wash the dishes. I ached to do actual labor, wanted to try, but the request was denied. Rejection. Only six months before I had fled dishpans for office.

Morning and afternoon I went to physiotherapy, pulling weights attached by leather bracelets to wrists and ankles. I walked for gait training, practiced stepping backwards, sideways or over objects. Several times a week I exercised in the Hubbard tank where the weightlessness of water made motion easier. Joe took me up several floors by elevator so I could practice walking down the steps. I moved slowly, gripped the railing, afraid of stumbling on the steel-edged concrete steps. Every day Joe walked me down halls, but he had to hold me for balance.

Getting down onto mats on all fours was a prerequisite to improved balance. The thought of opening my hands flat enough to bear weight on the palms was as painful as if I had been asked to drive a splinter under a fingernail. Joe brought two book-sized wooden blocks with handles that he placed beneath me on the floor. My spastic fingers clutched the handles. The first day I tried to balance on hands and knees, I shook with apprehension and weakness. A body harness suspended from an overhead frame kept me from falling on my face. Helplessness, the inability to catch myself if I toppled, was omnipresent and feared. Arms and legs shook and wobbled. "Don't. I'll fall. Take me down," I yelled.

"Stay there," Joe commanded.

He would not take me down until he was ready or until I had tried to stay as he put me. I remained on all fours only moments the first day, remembering my father hoisting sick horses with block and tackle attached to leather straps, in an effort to raise them to their feet. They had never recovered. Not me. Within a week I could remain on all fours five minutes without the harness, then ten minutes. The floor still looked hard and cruel. Fear of falling kept me frozen on hands and knees until I shouted that I was about to fall and Joe lifted me onto a chair to rest.

When I strengthened enough, I graduated to mat work. Joe lowered me onto the mats on my abdomen. He lifted first legs, then arms off the floor. I felt like a newborn colt finding its legs for the first time. I learned to crawl on hands and knees, a few feet farther each day until I crept the distance of two mats. Next it was backwards, then over pillows.

Sometimes I upset, rolled like a baby in a play pen, lurched on my face, struggled onto my abdomen. Joe lifted me onto all fours again. The most difficult lesson was learning to get onto hands and knees unassisted. I could draw my knees up with hips in knee-chest position, but I remained stuck in that undignified position with arms pinned under me. Getting onto my arms seemed impossible to coordinate. As soon as I moved to push up, I fell over and had to begin again.

When Joe had a day off, Craig, a younger, sterner therapist, supervised my gym time. "Get up!" he shouted. "Doctor Kaiser, get up! You can lie there all day until you get up." He left me, face down on the dusty mat, while he worked with other patients. My muscles fatigued if I struggled too long. Rest and try again. Finally I conquered the maneuver and struggled into crawl position. "Good," he said. "Now lie down and get up again. Once more before you can go back to your room." If I did fifteen or twenty sit-ups for Craig, he insisted on three more. I always returned to bed exhausted and slept until supper trays arrived.

"Don't you mind Craig shouting at you like that? It's terrible," one of the nurses who attended me on second floor said. "I heard Craig screaming at you from way down the hall." The gym doors were usually open for ventilation.

"No," I answered."It's his way of making me work hard. It's good for me. Besides, I like him. He's really a wonderful person."

With the intensive therapy and time, my wrists, hands and fingers never stopped hurting. I had fewer impulses flying down my arms ending in electric sparks at my finger tips. The most agony was in my back and shoulders until *TENS* was begun. Transcutaneous Nerve Stimulation is a rechargable battery pack connected to two electrodes taped to the skin. A constant mild electrical charge tingles between the electrode pads, relieving pain. Joe easily fastened the electrodes over my painful shoulders, but I had no shirt pocket to carry the cigarette-pack size battery. Finally, I carried it where I used to carry my beeper, nestled in the front of my bra.

When I returned to Community Hospital, Joe believed that he could reduce my finger swelling. My hands were still very limited in motion, also clumsy and swollen twice their usual size due to the nerve damage. At the end of afternoon therapy Joe applied a Jobst alternating pressure machine to both hands. My fingers returned to normal. Tight rubber surgical gloves were pushed on to maintain their reduced size, but after several hours the swelling returned and the nurses had to peel them off because of painful pressure. After a week's trial with no permanent reduction in finger size, we abandoned the experiment. I worried. Would my hands ever be useful again?

The third week of January a wonderful thing happened. It was of such great importance that its discovery remains as vivid as if it had been this morning. Keith, our older son who worked in Lancaster, came frequently over lunch hour to cut food to bite-size for my fork or to feed me soups. It was great to visit with him, and I appreciated the sacrifice of his lunch time. One noon after he had returned to work, I concentrated on hand motion. Suddenly, I could distinguish the slightest motion in my right thumb joint. "That's pretty definitive," physiotherapy agreed that afternoon. I thumbed my flag of victory to everyone I met.

Before long I noticed slight motion in all finger joints of the right hand. Many moments in my bed were spent attempting new mobility and strengthening regained ones. I thought how wonderful it would be if I could only rehabilitate enough to do my own housework from a wheelchair. I had known women who washed dishes or dusted from a wheelchair. I burned with the desire to accomplish menial activities that I had always hated. Daydreaming, I imagined pushing myself refrigerator to stove, preparing a meal. Our kitchen would need remodeling to accommodate work at this new level. I dismissed the fantasy remembering the promise that I would return to office and patients within a year.

Another day as I lay trying to slide my right arm along the sheet above my head, the hand moved high enough to touch my hair. Soon I was able to reach my call button and draw it within grasp if I was lying down, stretch for items on the bedside table, pick up the telephone if it was on the mattress beside me. At least I had one good arm. Each goal became a windmill to battle and conquer.

Drinking from a straw was easy, but I wanted to lift a glass. A nurse filled a styrofoam cup on my tray. Steadying the cup with my left hand, I wrapped the right hand around it. Pressure of the cup against my palm caused the hand to contract. The styrofoam cracked like an eggshell. A disaster of spilled milk on the tray. The next time I held the cup between clenched fists like a baby.

With improved finger function came the desire to hold regular forks and spoons, not ones bandaged into the hand, but I had forgotten how to hold them. It was like trying to manipulate chopsticks the first time. Awkward between my fingers, the tools dropped onto the tray. The nurse held a fork. I analyzed her grasp and imitated it. When my roommate was not looking, I watched her eat and practiced each mealtime until I could manage utensils again.

Success encouraged boldness. I ordered an apple for lunch. It sat on my tray through meat and potatoes, shiny, delicious looking, red. The smooth skin felt good in my hand. I wobbled the weight of it to my open mouth but could not press hard enough to break its skin for a first bite. The apple rolled away like a raindrop down a glass pane and fell onto the sheets. Disappointed at failure, too proud to ask for help, I added apples to my list of goals. The arms would get stronger.

I still wore diapers. "Drink at least eight glasses of fluids a day," nurses at the rehabilitation hospital had warned when I left them. Since most of my day was spent in therapy, I carried a sixteen-ounce glass of liquid with me, usually warm cranberry juice. After the accident, hypersensitivity to salt or cold made iced drinks difficult to swallow. Sipping liquids all day met the quota.

Catheterized every four hours for residual urine, taken regulary to the bathroom, I could not stay dry. Despite urine cultures and antibiotics, intermittent bladder infections plagued me month after month. Embarrassment and depression interfered with therapy. Sometimes I agonized and returned to my room, hiding my tears. I thought how even lowly caged animals had better bladder control.

Urinary tract X-rays were normal. The urologist's explanation of cord bladder was not new, but I had not applied the concept to myself. "A spinal-cord-injured bladder is smaller than before your accident. With contractile muscle innervation impaired, the bladder does not empty completely. The residual invites infection. When the bladder is full, it contracts and spills out urine. Of course the sphincter muscle that closes off the opening between bladder and urethra doesn't function in cord patients. Put yourself on a two hour schedule."

He did not say, "The rest of your life," but I understood. Mary Glick from Gordonville who wanted to marry despite incontinence, the Philadelphia man who carried a catheter in his hatband, medical school's half-awake drowsy afternoon lectures in urology and neurology snapped into unmuddied focus.

Reality must be accepted. My response to living with the problem was reducing the amount of fluids. I quit sipping juices all day and life became more bearable.

After my return to Community Hospital days flew with the speed of hummingbirds. February weekends were razored with cold and clothed in ice that crackled and splintered from the trees in glassy fragments. Snow mantled city streets, and the country roads drifted shut. Trips home were impossible.

During a blizzard nurses unable to go home or be replaced at shift changes bedded down in lounges. Several doctors moved into the hospital to care for emergencies. When the roads were still closed Monday, there was no therapy. The hospital seemed a castle surrounded by a moat of silent white streets. Patients and nurses spoke in hushed voices, as if some unknown disaster was about to tromp down the stark halls.

All patients who could be discharged from the hospital had gone home when the blizzard had been predicted. I had no roommate. Television became tiresome in large doses. I rode down corridors for exercise, watched the wandering drifts, felt the frigid air falling from heavy glass windows or walked my fingers over the bed to exercise my arms. Telephone calls to New Holland confirmed that my family waited out the storm and later that Pete and the boys were shoveling the driveway. The thought that this was one storm which had not called me to a birthing gave me smug satisfaction, but I wondered how many maternity cases had been airlifted to hospitals. How many ditches would have pulled me into their embrace, like the one near Ben and Sara's on a New Year's morning?

14

Ditched

Beginning the new year wheel-anchored in a country ditch, tired and awake too many hours, weary of night calls, wishing I were curled warm and comfortable beside my husband in our four-poster mahogany bed, thinking about the traditional sauerkraut and pork dinner I was expected to serve family and guests that evening was not my idea of starting anything new. It was not the way I would have planned it.

I turned off my engine to await a Good Samaritan with a strong push to unditch me and wondered what life might have been like if Father had allowed the farmer boy, Howard Georges, to court me. What if I had married him and his ninety-acre farm and had hands chafed by garden earth? What if I had a stable full of kids instead of a solo country practice? Would I now sit waiting for a chinook to melt the ice, coating the skin of mud under my Chevy's rear wheels?

The New Year's Eve party had been marked by conformity: the usual doctor associates with wives and friends, the expected complaints about hospital affairs, a little backbiting, midnight glasses raised and toasted, "Auld Lang Syne." One short hour in bed before Amishman, Ben Miller, telephoned to say that his wife's pregnancy was about ready for delivery. Please come to their farm. My head had throbbed. Eggnog and liver paté crawled up my gullet and furred my tongue like the coat on a muskrat.

The downhill of night was jet black with a matrix of drifting mist as I ascended Mountain Top Hill and crossed into Chester County, then north onto a potholed macadam road between Honeybrook and Morgantown. A turn left onto a winding black street, right at the crossroad, a left at a T until I drove east on narrow blacktop. Miller's bullet-pocked mailbox hung drunkenly over the road on a splintered post. Scrawled in a sloping freehand print, only *B   iller* could be seen on its rusted flank in the beam of my headlights.

The lane was frozen solid, but a warm December 31st had melted a thin coating of mud that stuck to my tires and rattled gravel-like hailstones under my fenders. I parked at the yard fence, pulled my coat tight against the creeping fog and stepped along the walk, edged by last week's shoveled snow, toward a rectangle of kitchen lamp-light tunneling the haze.

I entered the house through the family entrance, a washhouse tacked onto the old colonial home. Chester County has many old colonial houses, built in the early 1900s as summer homes for wealthy city families. Many of the houses were constructed around a wide central hallway. Above a cellar were four large rooms, one in each corner of the house. On the one side of the house were two parlor rooms; kitchen and dining room on the other. On the second floor there was a bedroom on each corner. These great houses of brick or frame were lipped with porches on two or three sides and shaded by benevolent maples. In the post-Victorian era when country estates dwindled, lands were subdivided and farmers moved into the mansions. Many old fireplaces were closed up or removed and the wooden porches torn away in the name of upkeep economy.

In the car I thought of walking for help, but there were no farms or houses nearby. Besides, the road was so slippery that I could not have walked far without falling. I tried again to pull out of the ditch but it was hopeless. I turned off the motor and waited, reviewing my visit to the Miller home.

Millers' house with twelve-foot ceilings and windows to the floor was a typical old Chester County house. I walked across worn kitchen linoleum to a front bedroom and imagined white-gowned ladies moving through the parlors, sipping tea on August porches. What would they say to the sagging floors, scarred cupboards, the boarded up fireplaces with stovepipes running across rooms to the chimneys? I warmed myself gladly at the bedroom space heater, knowing that necessity changes things.

Sara Miller was several hours from birthing. Ben pulled a rocking chair from the cold parlor across the hall into the bedroom. I rocked while Sara, draped in a homesewn pink housecoat, paced between her bed in the front room and the kitchen sink in the rear of the house. Her rounded shape slid grotesque shadows across the walls. She stopped to retie her muslin nightcap. "I hope this is over before the children get up," she said.

"Are their bedrooms heated?" I asked, glad to be inside on a cold night.

Sara laughed. "No. The three little ones sleep over the kitchen where it's warmer. Malinda and Annie are above us where this stovepipe goes through, but the boys sleep on the other side, even have their window open at night. They have plenty of quilts and sheet blankets too. They like it cold."

I shivered, considering a house without central heat. Later I took a flashlight, went out into the black frigid hall and up creaking steps along the chilly banister worn smooth by decades of sliding hands. Years after the house was built, the bathroom had been installed at the head of the stairs where the trunk and storage room had been located. A hissing Coleman lantern burned light into the cold bathroom. The hot and cold water spigots dripped a steady rhythm into tub and sink.

"Why the lantern in the bathroom?" I asked Ben when I returned to the warm bedroom. Flashlights are a necessary accompaniment to Amish bedrooms. The children did not need a lantern. "The faucets drip. You need new washers?"

Ben laughed. "No. A lantern throws a lot of heat. It keeps the pipes that go up through the cold hall from freezing. It sure is a mess if things freeze up. Same reason we let the water drip in the tub and sink." He brushed graying hair from his face and stroked his brown beard with a calloused left hand, his only hand. The right empty blue shirt sleeve was folded back and fastened with a safety pin above the elbow. He noticed me watching him.

From my ditched car I looked east for the first sign of dawn, but only black horizon seamed earth to sky. I switched on the engine to warm the car. The ditch still gripped my rear wheels. It was easy to sit and let my mind wander. Tragedy is a constant shadow of the farmer, children backed over by milk trucks, runaway horses in the fields, lost arms in corn pickers.

"That," Ben had said, lifting the stump in its sleeve, "that happened four years ago. Don't know what makes us farmers do such dumb things. Got it caught in a corn picker, like so many men do. Lost a lot of blood and time in the field at harvest. Good neighbors finished the fall work that year while I lay in the hospital. Guess I was impatient to get going instead of stopping the machine to unclog the fodder when it choked up. We men get mangled arms instead. Eh, Sara?"

But Sara was lying in bed, panting and pushing, her blue eyes squeezed shut and face swollen with effort. Within minutes she delivered a pudgy baby, her eleventh. I wiped mucus from its mouth, clamped and cut the cord before giving the squalling infant a cursory examination as I wrapped it in warm covers.

"Not as easy at thirty-nine as it was at twenty." Sara laughed snuggling her blanketed new son against jowled cheek. "The last boy should be named after his father. We'll call this one Ben." She winked at me, and I knew she hoped that this would be her last birthing. Happiness shone in her eyes and her smile, but fatigue lay in the lines of her face and the way she slumped into her pillow.

After bringing in the new year and sitting with the Millers, I was tired too. Catnaps under my corduroy coat in a pillowed rocking chair beside the Miller's space heater was a poor substitute for sleep in my own bed. I glanced at my watch; still time to get home for several hours between the sheets before my children awakened. I pulled a colorful Dresden plate quilt around Sara's shoulders. The birthing was over and cleaned up, the baby nearly an hour old and Ben would take charge until the teenage girls got up in several hours. Thirty minutes and I would be under my own quilts.

Outside, the air had become much colder. A cutting wind had whisked away the fog and focused stars into a myriad shimmering crystals. I trod the glazed walks as if they were glass bubbles. The car's wheels crunched through the icy skin on the lane, finding the mud beneath.

The black hardtopped road was grease slick. Studded tires did not grip the ice. I crept along steering into skids, glad that no cars shared the narrow byway. Then, after a mile or so, I veered slowly, gracefully, without control into the ditch as if the roadside's stubbled cornfield had swooped me into an embrace.

The ditch that held the rear wheels was not deep. My wheels spun, grinding into the berm, but the car slid sideways, not forward. One little push would have started me toward home again. Surely someone would pass soon. I slumped into my coat in the warm car, narcotized by wailing all-night country music on the radio.

I waited, tried again to climb out of the ditch. My car phone was useless with Mountain Top obstructing transmission. Dawn in an hour. No other cars drove by so early on a holiday.

Day birthed in the east, first like a lantern rising behind a hill, then like a red tongue that slowly rolled into a ball, throwing pink brilliance onto iced briar canes, wild cherry trees and corn stubble. No birds flew. No breeze broke the mystique of dawn or the icicles from the bushes. Only I seemed unsedated.

When the sun had pulled itself into a white fist of light above the horizon, the air warmed. I turned the key in the ignition and tried again to leave the ditch. It relented. The ice crust had softened. Spinning tires gripped the softened berm, and I slowly regained the blacktop, still as smooth as a baby's gums. The cindered main road descended the mountain to an iceless highway. I arrived in New Holland in time to get the family the bacon and egg breakfast I never served when I had to pull myself from bed to cook it.

15
Marriage

A s February turned to March and the days warmed toward spring, I imagined from my hospital bed the energetic hustle out in the countryside. Housewives would straddle fallow flower beds with teetering stepladders to wash winter's storms from the windows. The men would be pulling plows from sheds to dip their iron toes into the warming earth. Farm homes, bargained for over winter, would see their occupants moving like checkers on a board as growing families hunted more acreage and fledgling farmers settled their brides onto the land for a first season. Many young men hoped that the new life stirring under a wife's apron might be a boy to help with the milking and hauling manure. I expected that on spring days, Amish wagons mounded with beds and tables and chairs roped onto piled chairs moved along country roads.

Even Jake and Katie Fisher's little Mary must be old enough to be among the newly married. Several years ago the older couple had retired to the small frame end of his house when son John had married. I delivered babies now for John and Amanda in the back bedroom instead of for Jake and Katie, but vegetables still spilled from the roadside stand each summer. My first sighting of an Amish scarecrow had been in that garden.

There it was. I laughed to myself, had never considered the

possibility. Standing between a long row of string beans and a planting of sweet corn, an Amish scarecrow fluttered in Katie Fisher's faded blue dress. Its ample bosom and sun-streaked black bonnet were stuffed with straw that poked through the neck in an awesome yellow beard. Limp tattered skirts swayed lazily in August's heavy air. Two glittering aluminum pie pans dangled on strings from each end of the rough wooden stick that held ragged sleeves in a stiff inhuman pose.

Why not an Amish scarecrow? It was as natural as the considerate way that the Amish cared for their elderly, sick and handicapped. They were kept busy and needed, like Sarah Fisher, the patient I had come to see at Frogtown near the village of Intercourse.

I swung my station wagon around Jake and Katie Fisher's roadside vegetable stand. The wooden shack overflowed with cabbages, glossy purple eggplant, yellow and green peppers, carrots, green-topped beets, fresh bread and shoofly pies in plastic bags, eggs, jars of strawberry jam. Baskets of crimson tomatoes and pale-skinned potatoes sat on the ground beside a wheelbarrow of sweet corn, spilling unhusked onto a pile along the lawn.

The bushel of lima beans I had ordered would not be popular at my house. All hands had been warned to be ready for work when I returned home. The children hated lima bean sessions more than corn husking or pea shelling.

Fisher's gravel lane lay between the empty tobacco barn and a long vegetable garden. Leah, the oldest Fisher daughter at home, hoed a row of potatoes with a vigor no weed could survive. Mary bent over lima beans, filling a basket with the thick green pods. Her twin Sylvia, on hands and knees, weeded a long row of fragile young celery plants. The sisters wore pink short-sleeved dresses. They were barefooted. Their heads were covered by bandana handkerchiefs knotted at the nape of each neck below the hair bun. The girls waved. Leah nodded, walked past the weak-necked scarecrow and propped her hoe against the wire yard fence on her way to the house.

At other visits I had seen the girls push the reel mower that kept the Fisher yard looking as if it were manicured with a scissors. A brown ribbon of bare earth edged the walks to kitchen and wash-house, eliminating the need to clip grass along the concrete. Flower beds against the house were a profusion of geraniums, petunias and zinnias. Astors, delphiniums and dahlias bloomed along the fence and continued to a bed of impatiens and varigated coleus on the sunless north side of Sarah's wing of the house.

"Hello Sarah," I called, entering her cool shaded room through the screened door. The east and west shutters were closed against the sun. "What are you working at today?"

She smiled. "This is green day. Mary poured a new batch of animals for me yesterday." Twisted knobby fingers gripped a small brush wet with green paint. On the newspaper-covered table, plaster chickens, cows, horses, pigs and ducks stood on freshly painted grass. "This work keeps me busy. Seems I can never keep up with the orders." Sarah fumbled the lid onto the jar.

Sarah Fisher had been disabled several years before I began routine house calls. Once a teacher in an Amish school, she had to retire because of severe arthritis which had finally limited her to bed and wheelchair.

Sarah's youngest brother Jake had added an ell to his house. A bachelor brother Jonas, who talked with a lisp when he spoke, which was seldom, slept upstairs. Jonas paid board at Jake's table helping him at harvest time. He worked nights catching chickens for Victor F. Weaver, Inc. in New Holland. I rarely saw the rotund and rusty-bearded middle-aged man.

Sarah was always home, except during times she visited her eleven younger siblings. Home was at Jake's. Katie and the older girls were accustomed to Sarah's care and took turns sleeping on a cot in her room. Even attending church was impractical and painful for Sarah. She only attended when the Fishers took their annual turn to host the district's church service.

"This is my week to care for Aunt Sarah," Leah said, wiping garden dirt from her toes onto the doormat. "I like to help over here." The girl washed her hands at a corner sink. "Have her in bed in a minute."

Leah's slim body moved with grace and the skill of her work. She pushed Sarah's wheelchair to the bed, hooked the canvas backsling and seat to the hydraulic lift, deftly pumped the handle and swung her patient over the bed. Pressure released, Sarah's thin rigid body rested on the log cabin quilt. Sarah grimaced when her niece straightened her black dress and apron, pulling out folds under hips and shoulders.

A wrinkled, child-size little woman lay on the bed. Her white cap, fastened to a narrow black band by a straight pin at the midline part, emphasized the thin white hair. Black-stockinged legs maintained sitting position. Sarah clutched a white handkerchief in knotted fingers.

Finished with my patient, I turned to Leah. "Leah, that's a big celery patch in your garden." I imagined fall with the rows of celery bleached and protected from frost by mounded earth and covered with long rolls of plastic. "Your family going to eat it all, or is there a November wedding?"

My victim turned away, pretending to examine the plaster animals. "Takes a lot of celery for this family. You're just guessin'. I'm twenty-two. That's old enough to marry." She brushed dust from her skirt and leaned against the white wall. Her brown eyes and lean face were innocent. "Besides, wouldn't need to be me. Could be the twins."

No confession from Leah. Most Amish marriages do not become public knowledge until the banns are announced in church about a month before the wedding and long rows of marriage licenses with traditional Amish names begin appearing in autumn newspapers.

During our early years in New Holland Pete and I often passed through the village of Intercourse Sunday evenings to see the Amish young folks gather. Many came to the triangle in front of the bank and went from there to the evening sing held in the home of a friend. We watched horses pulling open courting buggies, clogging the streets. Sometimes the skittish animals tempted their drivers to race. We watched brothers drive sisters to the gatherings, two sitting on the seat, the third passenger astride the middle knees of those on the bottom. We watched the young men with their girlfriends, knowing they would escort them to the singing, then take them home, often not arriving at their own homes until morning milking time.

***

"Leah wants to marry this fall," Katie said at the October prenatal visit. "Last year it was Sallie. She's expecting early December; me in the middle of November. Problem is setting a date for Leah's wedding." She grinned a dentured smile that deepened wrinkles under blue eyes and along her cheeks. "Guess you can't say yet if I'll be early or late?"

I shook my head. "At least you have plenty of help with eleven at home yet."

Katie exposed her sagging abdomen for examination. "I'll be able to boss them." She shifted to sitting position with a long grunt. "Little Jake is two. Time we had another baby to spoil. Guess this'll be our last. Thought so last time." Slender fingers searched the depths of a voluminous blue tapestry bag and found a man's pocket watch. "Time to get home for dinner. Jake went to Kauffman's Hardware for nails and caulking. Guess he's waiting out back at your hitching rail." Katie turned at the door. "Would you and your husband like to come to Leah's wedding?"

I felt honored to be invited to an Amish wedding. By tradition they are held on Tuesdays and Thursdays. Tuesday allows Monday for washing, cleaning up and catching up with chores after Sunday. Wednesday is a day to work after Tuesday's activity and prepare for Thursday. Thursday ceremonies allow Friday and Saturday to work and prepare for a day of rest on Sunday. During wedding season folks often brag about their number of wedding invitations, and only essential work is done around farm and home.

Amish church rules require that a bishop officiate the wedding ceremony. This limits the number of weddings per day and if there are many weddings that year, requires some marriages to fall into late October or early December. November customarily lies between the work of corn picking and tobacco stripping. Fall weddings allow families to prepare young couples for housekeeping in March when farms become available. Widows and widowers, in their need to restore family life, marry any time of the year.

In addition to the Tuesday and Thursday limitations, families maneuver dates to avoid conflicts with weddings of cousins and friends as well as family birthings. Jake and Katie set Leah's wedding for late November hoping to beat Sallie's baby and have Katie's birthing past by several weeks.

The first week in November Jake called me to Frogtown. "Can you stop near the cheese plant on the way over and pick up Mommy

Glick? We'll need a granny."

It was after midnight but Katie's mother, slipper-footed and dress unpinned, climbed onto my front seat only minutes after I knocked on her kitchen door. There had been no time to pack her bulging green tapestry bag. I never stopped for a granny who did not come with a bag of cookies, a jar of fresh jam and the craving to be included in the action of new birth. "I didn't want to keep you waiting. Katie might need us. Remember how fast she went with little Jake? I've had this bag packed for the last week or so."

Rachel Glick managed to tug on black stockings and shoes as I rounded curves and bounced potholes, added straight pins to finish closing her dress and cape over a matronly bosom. She pinned a narrow black cotton ribbon around her head and with a straight pin fastened her organdy cap to it at her central part. After the black hardboard bonnet covered her white hair, she settled against the seat and seemed ready to be granny. That meant receiving the new baby into warm blankets, dressing it and staying with the family to care for Katie until a maiden Amish woman came as nurse. Rachel would fetch a basin, old rags and baby clothes, then sit and tell me of her eight birthings, her multitude of grandchildren and how Amish folk from Quarryville to Lititz were doing, while we awaited Katie's birthing.

By 4:30 a.m. when Jake called the boys downstairs for morning feeding and milking, Katie hugged a new daughter in her arms. "Little Katie," Jake said. "Katie G. Fisher."

Leah and Mary came down to admire the baby, then fried mush and eggs for breakfast. Amos, John and Ezra put on old coats from hooks behind the space heater, pushed work-stained wool hats on their heads and went to the barn. Sylvia came from Sarah's room to hold the baby, then carried it back to her aunt for approval before helping little Martha and toddler Jake button clothes and tie shoestrings.

"Now all we have to think about is Sallie holding off until after Leah's wedding," Katie said, looking at a calendar on the bedroom wall.

***

Leah G. Fisher and Levi B. Ebersole were married the Tuesday
after Thanksgiving. I could not spare time from morning office hours
to sit through services that began at eight and lasted until noon and I
would not have understood the High German. My afternoon was
needed for patient rounds. Pete and I agreed to attend supper and
the evening sing. We arrived at four o'clock, waiting at the end of the
lane to drive to the house. Families leaving the wedding to go home
for evening feeding and milking clogged the lane. Carriages
stretched toward South Queen Street in a gray undulating ribbon. At
the barn teenage hostlers helped hitch and unhitch horses to the
wagons that dotted the pasture beside the stable like raisins in a
pudding. Horses were tied in the stable and along the second floor of
the barn between the haymows and beneath unstripped tobacco,
hanging on laths along scaffolding that rose to the barn peak.

Pete and I parked between a large black van and the gray bench
wagon that stored and transported the folded benches of a church
district. A dozen shawled and bonneted girls and jacketed boys ran
in the yard. Clusters of men in black overcoats and wide-brimmed
black hats stood about talking. They said "Hello" or nodded as we
passed to the kitchen door.

The Fisher yard had been combed of stray leaves, summer's
flower beds cleaned of every brown frozen stalk. The boarded-up
vegetable stand looked cold and bare against the empty garden. I
wondered where the scarecrow had gone. The earth lay dark and
fallow until spring. A straw bale covered each cellar window keep-
ing winter winds from the house. The large front porch had been
enclosed with plastic sheeting. Through it I could see benches for
extra seating and two cupboards moved from the house.

A wall of hot air bearing odors of cooked onions and celery, roast
chicken and the stuffiness of a crowd met us at the open door. The
Fisher house had changed. The stone farmhouse had always seemed
large, but on this wedding day it rivaled the barn floor. The varnished wooden partitions between Jake and Katie's bedroom, the
parlor, the large kitchen, even into Sarah's frame end of the house,
had been removed to make one large room. Beds had been taken
down, bureaus and cupboards taken out or pushed against the wall.
Parlor rugs were gone exposing wide pine boards. Only the usual
three space heaters remained. I wondered if they were needed or if

the knurls of black-garbed women sitting about chatting in Pennsylvania Dutch would have warmed the room. A great U of tables, covered with a variety of cloths, encircled the room.

Katie came to greet us, changing from Pennsylvania Dutch to English. "Glad you got here. We'll have supper soon."

I had seen many of Katie's and Jake's sisters and the neighbor women in my office. As married women they wore a Sunday dress, cape, black apron and a white cap. They smiled and offered a chair. One woman held a baby girl. Amish mothers wore dresses similar to their own on babies when they brought them to my office, but I had only heard of nearly bald infant girls wearing white caps to church and was amazed the tiny child did not pull it off. She did manage to get its wide strings into her mouth. Because of the large number of adults invited to weddings, only children of the bride's and groom's immediate family or nursing infants could attend.

I greeted Katie, Sarah, then the other women with a handshake. Sarah looked happy surrounded by friends and family. I wondered how many pain pills she had taken that day, how many plaster animals she had sold, how many orders she had taken for Christmas.

"Jake and I don't work today," Katie said. "But you can see everybody has been busy this week. Yesterday we scrubbed three washtubs of celery. The best goes to the bride's table. We cooked fifty chickens and ducks, cut them up with the bread for the roast. Mary and Sylvia made two lard cans of applesauce Friday. Neighbor Henry Beilers made all the doughnuts." Katie accepted my wedding gift, a nest of bowls, and handed them to a young girl.

"Get Sylvia to take you to the cellar to see all the cakes. Leah's girlfriends decorated cakes with fancy icing and nuts. Some have figures of barns, fences, animals and people. We'll freeze the ones we don't eat today. Mary and Sylvia put colored candies and nuts in the secret wedding cake they baked." Katie stopped to shake hands with newcomers in black shawls.

"Too bad you couldn't get here this morning. We sang, the ministers spoke. Last came the marriage ceremony by Bishop Daniel Stoltzfus, then Levi and Leah went upstairs until some benches were made into tables and the rest used to sit on. When they came down, they were happy to see the different cakes, nuts and fruit at the *Eck*, the special corner of the table where bride and groom are served."

I nodded to Katie, trying to absorb everything she said, comparing it to weddings in our culture. When Pete and I were married, Mother, Grandmother and I had made platters of crustless fancy sandwiches, made punch and bought ice cream to go with the baker's wedding cake. "Glad I don't have to manage and prepare food for three or four hundred people. And two meals. Guess you're glad for any help you can get."

Katie continued, "The week before the wedding an Amish groom comes to the bride's house to help work, so we had Levi here to help out. Tomorrow Levi and Leah will clean up and do the wash if the children here will let them. Leah's brothers and sisters will tease them, tie the tablecloths in knots, dump out the wash water. It will be a lively place. I think Levi hid the washing machine so nobody could steal the gasoline engine or wringer.

"This afternoon a bunch of girls tricked Leah into jumping over the broom so she's a *Hausfrau* now. They were going to sew her fork and knife fast to the tablecloth but they got caught. Jake heard Levi's friends say they were going to throw him over the fence to the married men. Don't know if they got it done.

"Tonight you and your husband will sit at a special table with others who just came for the evening meal. You'll be served leftovers from the noon meal along with supper."

Pete sat across the table from me with the men. Ivan Smucker, a Mennonite from Nine Points, sat beside him. Ivan, a retired farmer, had driven his black van full of Amish neighbors to the wedding. Frequently, for extra income, retirees rented time and transportation to buggy-driving folks, charging a set price per mile per person. "This is the third wedding my passengers have been to today," Ivan said. "I drove to Christ Zooks at Georgetown for the service and noon meal, stopped at John Riehls near Skelp Level this afternoon and now here for supper."

The tables were set with a mismatch of metal plates and stainless steel flatwear in a variety of patterns. Later Mary told me that they belonged to the church district and were kept in a chest to be used for church, weddings and funerals. Water glasses were plain, printed, octagonal, tall, short and even some jelly glasses. I wondered if the neighbors had contributed theirs for the day.

Everyone bowed their heads for silent grace. We lifted them to a slice of bread on each plate. As if a starting gun had sounded, a network of flailing arms reached for jam and butter to spread on the staff of life. Dishes of roast, gravy, creamed celery, beans, coleslaw, chowchow, noodles, chips, mashed potatoes, pickles and fruit salad rushed past. Supper's menu also moved hand to hand along the table. Raw celery, doughnuts, cornstarch pudding, cookies, cake, pie, ham, macaroni and cheese, all dished onto the same plate. We were overwhelmed. This was no time for gawking or talking. If anything impressed me, it was the speed with which food was shoveled into mouths. I had never seen anything like it. Within minutes it was over. My plate was not empty when hands around me rubbed crumbs from beards and chins.

Those who served tables were friends of the newlyweds who had married the year before. Several women carried unmistakable bulges beneath their aprons; others I knew had small babies in a bedroom upstairs.

We bowed our heads in another silent grace and rose from the benches to make room for the next seating. We found chairs along the wall. Two galvanized laundry tubs on casters, one with suds, one with hot rinse water, were rolled to the center of the room. The helpers, men and women alike, washed, rinsed and dried dishes at a furious rate, resetting the tables as they worked. Others refilled empty serving dishes. Katie said there had been more than three settings at the noon meal; two fed everyone at supper.

The young folks had come in from the tobacco stripping room and barn, where they had been socializing, and gone upstairs to wait until they were invited to come down for supper. We watched as the bride and groom emerged from the upstairs door and walked to the bride's corner. I expected Leah to have a special bride's dress, but she wore a new navy blue one made in the style of all her other dresses. Levi wore a new black Sunday suit. As a married woman Leah would now wear a black apron to church instead of the white one worn by single girls.

Next the two young men and two young women, who were the attendants, descended the stairs hand-in-hand. The bride and groom and these attendants had spent the late afternoon hours pairing the remaining young folks, usually asking for both the boy's and girl's consent. These couples now also came down the stairsteps holding hands and filed to seats along the heavily laden supper table. We visited while the young folks ate.

I wondered how Katie managed everything: dowry furniture, rugs, quilts over the years, the wedding, even a baby scarcely a month old. Last year daughter Sallie was married; now Leah; more daughters to marry in years to come. Jake and Katie should be glad that half their children were sons. Would Pete and I have fewer responsibilities, or only different ones? I chewed a pretzel and took an apple from snacks passed around after everyone was fed and thought of our children's college years ahead, our daughters' weddings.

The pleasure of the evening sing with the young couples joining in rounded out the happy occasion. Sallie handed Pete and me an Amish hymnal. I do not know what we sang, each verse begun by a leader, the wedding guests joining him in a singsong chanting wail without musical accompaniment. I knew enough German to follow the singers and mutter a few words. All tunes sounded alike as I blundered along. I looked at Sallie. She laughed at me. Others grinned and I laughed too.

When women began climbing the stairs to sort out black bonnets and shawls with their initials embroidered on the corner, and the men slipped on heavy black overcoats and wool hats, Pete and I thanked our hosts. We shook hands and left amid the carriage traffic. We were home by eleven o'clock.

If there was any lesson learned that Tuesday after Thanksgiving, it was that if I should ever again be invited to an Amish wedding, I would eat faster and not miss the cherry pie that passed me by, making room for it on my plate amid the roast and gravy.

***

Snow patched the hollows of fields and lay in dirty black ribbons along the roadsides where it had been thrown up by last week's plows when I visited Sarah Fisher on January's foggy morning. It was a long-awaited wet day that allowed laths of fragile brown tobacco to be taken down from their scaffolding and placed in the damp room beside the stripping room.

The stripping room in the basement of the tobacco barn was a busy place as I drove past its windowed front. Jake, with sons and daughters too old to be in school, pulled the finger-staining tobacco leaves from stalks and laid them in piles to be pressed into paper-wrapped bales. Mary saw me and waved as I walked toward Sarah's room.

The windows in Sarah's space heater glowed red from the burning coals that radiated comforting heat into the room. Odors of freshly baked bread or cake filtered into the room from Katie's kitchen beyond the varnished partition. I recognized Leah's and Katie's voices in muffled bits of laughter and conversation in the next room.

"It's my week to help Aunt Sarah," Mary said, removing her jacket and scarf. "Sylvia works three days a week making jam at Kitchen Kettle and Leah is pretty busy these days." She lowered Sarah onto her bed.

Katie opened a door in the partition, held flour-covered hands in mid-air. A blast of spices, apples and cooking meat came in with her. "When you're finished with Sarah, come over to our side if you can spare a minute. Something I want to show you." She hesitated, directed her attention to her daughter. "Mary, can you help here in the kitchen until dinner?"

Finished with Sarah, I entered Katie's kitchen. Cloves and cinnamon surged from the black gas stove oven as Leah removed a tray of brown-rimmed buttermilk cookies, knobby with nuts and raisins. "Our boys like their sweets," Katie said, offering me a cookie the size of a doughnut. "Mary, can you change the baby then mash the potatoes?"

I resolved to add Katie's recipe to those from other Amish kitchens as my teeth sank into the soft warm cookie. "What is the dough hanging on the wooden clothes rack?" I watched Katie roll out the last large paper-thin oval on the kitchen table and hang it to dry before rinsing her hands at the sink.

"I'm making noodles. Later when they're dry I'll take the noodle cutter, finish them off and store them in cans. Leah will need some too when she goes to housekeeping." Katie shook her head. "Trouble is Jake wants the girls to help finish the tobacco stripping, and I need them in the house. Sold his tobacco for a good price this year, took the last of it down this morning. Soon as stripping is over, we have a pile of sewing ahead."

"What do you have on the wire racks?" I asked, examining dried up, brown nubbins in a three-layered homemade dehydrator on the back of the space heater.

Mary laughed. "Taste one. Dried apple snitz for snitz pies. About dry enough to put away now. We cook them to a sauce with sugar, cinnamon and cloves for a two-crusted pie that we serve when it's our turn for church. Ever have a snitz pie?"

I nodded, savoring the chewy apple lump. A mouthful could occupy a person most of an evening. A snitz pie was a real treat.

Katie dried her hands and turned down the gas under a chattering kettle. "I called you over to show you the parlor. Come see."

The air in the unheated parlor was damp and heavy with the odor of varnish, harness oil and new things. Katie's green couch and rocking chairs, with their bright needlepoint cushions, had been pushed against the wall beside the Dutch cupboard and drop-leaf table. Trestle and board tables occupied the space between a dismantled bed and six new kitchen chairs painted with clusters of fruit on their glassy varnish.

"Leah's *Hausschteier*," Katie said, sweeping an arm over the tables of pots, pans, nests of bowls, stainless flatwear, hand-painted dishes, mirrors and a plywood letter rack. A stack of embroidered tea towels and pillow cases lay between dishcloths and sheets still in plastic wrappings. "That other table is Levi's things." She pointed to hammers, several saws, a bridle, a pair of reins, two oil cans, buckets and more than my eyes and brain could catalogue.

"Wedding gifts? I didn't see these at the wedding."

"No. We Amish don't bring gifts to a wedding. Until March when their rented farm will be free, Leah lives at home like usual during the week. Levi stays as hired man for his brother Daniel K. Zook at Buena Vista. Ever since the wedding Levi picks Leah up Friday evenings, and they visit around at wedding guests' houses and get the wedding gifts. Uncle Amos R. Glicks gave them that nice mantle clock. Levi brings her back home Sunday nights."

I knew that Amish women liked nice china. "Do they have a set of good dishes?"

"Levi gave them to her the Christmas before they were married. It's almost like an engagement gift."

We both knew of Leah's early pregnancy with its morning nausea but did not discuss it. "Do people know they're coming for dinner, spending the night and collecting a wedding gift?"

"Oh yes. We know when to expect young folks. We've been working all winter scraping, varnishing and polishing old bureaus, tables and chairs, getting them ready for Leah and Levi. Bought most of them at sales. Got Leah her own sewing machine coupla years ago. Handy to have several in the house. Mary and Sylvia have them too."

"What does Levi's family do?"

"They help them get started farming. Levi's brother Isaac is moving off the sixty-acre farm their dad bought near Nickel Mines so Levis can move in. Levi's mother made him several quilts too."

"It sure takes a lot to get started."

"Yes. Cows, horses, plows and machinery to buy yet too. It was the same for Jake and me. We took Leah's last quilt out of the frame a week ago. Had a quilting bee for my sisters, then Jake's sisters after Christmas to get it finished.

"Everything finished now?"

"All but the carpets. We keep all the men's old shirts and the girls dresses, tear them in strips, sew them end to end, stitch the edges in and roll them in balls. We took them to Big Ben Beiler at Leaman Place, but he is so busy looming rugs this time of year. Guess Leah will be without rugs awhile. She can use the hooked ones she made. We'll have the infare in two weeks. That's when the groom's family invites Leah's whole family to dinner."

Last year Katie and Jake had gone through this process with Sallie. This year it was Leah. Next year it could be Mary, Sylvia or even a double wedding, and way down the years little Katie.

Aunt Sarah had watched November pass November. Was it by her choice that she never had a wedding, never had collected a *Hausschteier*?

16

Ripples and Reflections

After four weeks of hospital confinement by weather, March came to me as a welcome change. Its warmer days unfolded toward April, like the blue and white crocuses blooming on our New Holland lawn. Finally, I saw weekends at home again.

Not that I was bored or lonely in the hospital. Therapy occupied most of the day, family and friends came to visit, frequent telephone calls kept me in touch with the outside world. But phone calls were stormless waves in comparison to the, "hurry over my wife's having her baby now," or the humorous and jaunty calls I had received during the years of practice. I laughed remembering the 5:00 a.m. raspy voice that panted, "Can you come over right away? I got a cow down with mastitis. Wanted to get ya before I started milkin'." The caller did not give his name but the throaty voice was unmistakably Jake Riehl's. He had called every time his wife Malinda had birthed one of their seven children. We had spent hours in the Riehl's warm kitchen, chewing over intolerable milk inspectors, the quality of that season's hay and tobacco prices. I knew Jake's voice.

"You want the vet," I told the excited Amishman, fumbled the phone back into its cradle and hunted the warm hollow under the covers. I envisioned Jake in his ragged barn clothes and stained straw hat, squinting deep-set blue eyes, scanning the graffiti of scrawled names and numbers in a telephone shanty hanging over a road bank someplace east of Churchtown. The waning yellow flashlight beam had not distinguished the vet's name amid the overwritten jumble of names.

Another day Josiah Glick called, concerned about his newborn son's unhealed umbilicus. Josiah's name had not sounded familiar, even in a community in which the names on mailboxes were duplicated many times.

"Did I deliver your baby?" I searched my memory for the recent delivery.

"No," Josiah answered. He hesitated, laughed nervously. "We didn't have you for the baby. The vitamin salesman that comes around regular delivered it. Didn't cost as much. He did it for just a donation."

Too often people carried health and illness in their pocketbooks. I sighed, shuddered and gave Josiah's baby an appointment. I rarely scolded a patient for delaying visits, for using home poultices or for seeking help from a donation-fee, self-educated country healer. Instead I listened.

Lecturing patients about overdosing on expensive vitamins and health concoctions, self-treating wounds or delaying prenatal visits would only have blurred case histories, and I would not have learned that *salva* (sage) tea, available in most home gardens, helps diarrhea. I would not have heard that before calling a physician for a child's earache, a father might blow tobacco smoke in its ear to relieve pain.

When Elsa our oldest child was small, I took her with me so frequently on house calls that it became part of the visit. "Guess what Mary and Sadie were playing yesterday?" Susie Stoltzfus said in my office. She smiled, remembering her daughter's antics. "Doctor Kaiser and Elsa on a house call. Mary was you. Sadie was Elsa and she pulled her along by the hand. They pretended to examine a doll."

Sliding a stethoscope along a wheezing chest could coat scope and fingers with tarry Ichthymol or pink Antiphlogistine's gummy paste. A spoonful of Great Find was used to cure innumerable ailments. Pregnant mothers rubbed Mother's Friend over their abdomens to prevent stretch marks, or they drank raspberry leaf tea for easier delivery of the placentas. If home remedies did not conflict with acceptable medical treatment, I shared the case with tradition.

In the hospital I enjoyed the visits of friends, like the evening three Amish ladies, Annie Stoltzfus, Ruth Fisher and Hannah Beiler, hired a driver and came to visit.

Annie and Ruth unloaded their black bonnets and shawls onto the vacant bed beside mine. Annie pulled an unfinished pillow case from her voluminous bag, plucked a needle from the fabric and began to embroider. Ruth's hand emerged from her tapestry tote with a new shirt for her husband. She began to stitch buttonholes.

Hannah sat as if afraid to remove her wraps. "Guess what I have?" she said, her brown eyes bright in a round face. She dimpled with a secret she could not wait to reveal. Beneath her shawl, her right arm bulged with an obvious package. Slowly, she lifted the black wool. A small dark shape lay on the crook of her arm. "Thought the nurses might not let me bring this in to show you." The infant wore a tiny blue bonnet and a black shawl over her pink dress, white stockings and booties. "Her name's Malinda."

Another day a group of Amish ladies, who completed a beautiful Texas star quilt in shades of blue, spread it across the vacant bed beside mine. I had delivered at least one baby for each woman, some with special experiences. The quilt was admired by hospital personnel and visitors before I sent the love gift home. I resolved to invite the quilters to New Holland for ice cream and cake when I was discharged.

There were other ways in which I felt special. On my birthday the hospital administrator and the dietitian, an old acquaintance who shared my birth year and month, marched into my room with a candled cake. I never learned who wore the white pile skin at Easter when a giant rabbit hopped into therapy and handed me a basket of candy eggs. One day Joe and I had our pictures taken for the hospital newspaper.

Joe still spent evenings with me when he was in town. He stressed the importance of a good diet to gain strength, told me how to move up in bed when I slid down. I learned to cover myself by gripping the sheet with my teeth. If ever I write about my hospital days, I will title the book *Hang on to Your Teeth 'Cause You Can't Gum the Bed Sheets.*

If another patient occupied the other bed in my room, time moved faster. We talked and watched television together. During February when I could not get home, I became hooked on football. Over and over my roommate and I saw tangles of heaped and twisted bodies unravel, marveling that the gladiators got onto their feet to regroup and clash again. The thuds and grunts as hurling bodies met bodies, the clunk of helmet on helmet, made me wince as I remembered the force and orange shock of my fall. I wondered how even seasoned men could survive impact after impact and was thankful my sons were not football players.

We roommates cheered the teams and held our breaths as yardage was measured for a first down or players struggled on the one-yard line as the clock ran out. Some weeks saw more warriors than others limp from the field or hauled off on stretchers. At one game, when a favored player was carried off, it was announced that he had a possible spinal cord injury. During the next Sunday's game the diagnosis of quadriplegia was confirmed. The hero's name was never mentioned again. He was just one more number among the 10,000 spinal cord injuries a year in the United States. It was as though he had never existed. I knew that his future had been snapped like a whip from under him. After possible surgery for fracture of his neck and months of physical rehabilitation, life in a wheelchair lay before him. The most important and difficult change would be adjusting from a life of activity and fame to one of oblivion and anonymity.

The game's announcer did not elaborate whether the injured player was married. If he was single, I imagined anguished parents rushing across the country, travel and hotel at their expense. There would be anxious hours and days as he rehabilitated, unexpected responsibility for a son they believed gone from the nest. If he had a wife and children, their futures would be altered forever. Many marriages do not survive the change. Some wives cannot endure a husband unable to embrace them or make love to them as before the accident. The possibility of fathering children is dim.

I thought about my former roommates at City, how Jimmy's parents had changed their hopes for his future, built a wheelchair-accessible wing to their home. Cindy's nursing career had ended at midpoint. Every evening during visiting hours her bed had been surrounded by concerned parents and friends.

While attention is focused on the injured, families spend a multitude of hours and many dollars traveling to and from the hospital, depriving themselves of valuable time. They wonder what the future holds, worry that they act and plan properly under the cloud that has suddenly cast its dark shadow over everything they do.

My family passed under that long shadow the night of my injury. After I was loaded into the ambulance, Pete drove to New Holland to tell our sons, Keith and Paul, what had happened to me before driving to the hospital. "The longest drive in my life," he said later. He did not return to the campground to help with the festival weekend we had planned. The next day Pete and Paul folded the trailer and took it home.

Our camping friends were upset and concerned by the accident. Pete telephoned Elsa in Denver and she called her sister Lorelei, a freshman in college several blocks away. Disbelief, a desire to fly home, then a more practical wait-and-see attitude followed. How fortunate that our children were grown and no longer mother-dependent. The days of ball games, school concerts, PTA were past. I had been den mother for the boys. Camped Girl Scouts to Washington, Colorado and Wyoming.

Keith had returned home to live after college. Paul was a high school junior. Always independent, now he became more so. During my first weeks in the hospital he visited to complain about the battered Toyota with unstylish torn upholstery that I had bought for Lorelei and him to drive to work at Red Run Campground. His eyes glowed with desire as he told me about the wonderful Bradley GT car in the garage of his scoutmaster. "Sorry, Paul," I said. "I'm in no position to help you. But, if you can sell the old car and swing the deal without additional funds, the Bradley is yours." Paul matured as he advertised, then sold the Toyota, as he worked hours getting the Bradley road-ready.

We learned months after the October 13th accident that there were speculations our marriage would not endure the crisis, that Pete would tire of my change from independence to complete helplessness. I never gave the idea a moment, assumed he would be at my side as I had supported him during his three hospital months and recuperation when he had had a leg masticated to kibble by a backhoe at our Spring Gulch Campground.

It is not always easy to be a doctor's husband. At times he is expected to pass out free medical advice or give inside information regarding the life of his wife. The myth that doctors, by reason of their profession, are affluent, prospering at the expense of victimized patients, overshadows the need for a husband to earn a living. He is sometimes seen as living in the luxurious lap of his wife.

Pete was crushed, literally and emotionally, soon after my hospitalization. An Amazon, a nursing supervisor, cornered him, her large arms and huge body stapling him into a corner. "I'm so sorry about your wife's accident. What ever will your family do now? How will you get along?" She did not release her grip on the wall until he assured her that the Kaisers were not headed for the county poor house. He hurried down the corridor without telling her that since college he had never been without a job. Why bother? She had injured his ego and no hospital insurance compensated for that.

At home in New Holland reorganization kept the wheels oiled and turning. After the weekly cleaning lady washed the dirty laundry, dusted the chairs and swept the floors, there was only grocery shopping and the evening dinner to appease three male appetites. Pete was no cook. He had often laughed and bragged that a clause in our wedding certificate stated that providing meals was my wifely duty.

Pete's mother to the rescue. Oma, at seventy-eight, took on the responsibility of planning, shopping and supper. Every day at three o'clock she crossed our backyards to begin the evening meal. After cooking only for herself the past twenty years, she was flabbergasted at how much food three hungry men could eat and worried about the total at the checkout counter.

When tragedy strikes, it stirs up not only one ripple but is like a stone skipped across a pond, producing multiple ruffles. I lay in the hospital remembering obligations. The first week of hospitalization a nurse dialed numbers and held the telephone against my head while I unburdened duties.

When the obstetrical group of doctors assumed my office hours and hospital cases until a permanent physician could be found, it relieved a great responsibility. Patients expecting home births had to hunt other physicians. Patients at term or with special problems requiring house calls occupied my thoughts. I had let them down, abandoned them. I wondered how they felt.

At Community Hospital a substitute had to be found for the staff office I was to assume. I deserted hospital committees that had occupied time and thought. A stack of charts became weeks overdue until brought to my bedside at City Rehabilitation Hospital for completion.

The capable vice president of the County Parks Board assumed my responsibilities and became its next president. I remained an active member until I left Lancaster County.

In the village of Terre Hill a men's prayer group met weekly for breakfast in the back room of a restaurant. They placed me on their prayer list, one of many prayer chains and lists composed by local friends and cousins from New Jersey to Florida.

Patients and friends stopped during a day's activities to visit me in the hospital or send a card. Pete visited regularly, seldom missing a day. He, Keith, Paul or a friend opened and read each card. Many contained notes. I enjoyed cards from Amish and Mennonite friends who took the time to write detailed letters describing the weather, what the housewife prepared for the next meal, how garden and field crops fared. Often they contained lists of their children with birth years, indicating the ones I had delivered.

***

By mid-March, five months after the accident, I was stronger and able to wash and feed myself, use the telephone, move in bed and sit on its edge unassisted. I could not walk without help.

"Let's use a walker," Joe said. "But only if someone is with you."

Another step toward independence. Someone still had to stand me up before I could take a step. My hands on the walker gave me stability but my left arm was not strong. Evening nurses took me for walks in the hall. The walker period was brief.

"Now we'll go to Canadian crutches." Joe pulled me to my feet and slipped my forearms through the U-shaped supports. I grasped both handles. The right hand held firm and lifted the crutch as I stepped forward with the left foot, but the weak left hand slipped its hold. The crutch fell away. Joe taped the hand to the crutch and I moved across the gym, right crutch and left foot forward, left crutch with the right foot. The rhythm came easily, but I worried about falling and was glad that Joe stayed close in case I lost balance. By the next therapy period a wide strap had been glued to the left crutch. Velcro held the insecure left fist tight to the handle. The wheelchair remained my daytime residence, the Canadian crutches became my means of walking. After I fell crossing an alfalfa field one weekend, my concern grew about not being able to shuck my arms free when I tumbled. A forearm fast in a crutch might mean a sprained or broken arm. Several months later I graduated to a cane.

It was time to think of going home more than weekends, a necessity when my hospital insurance came to an end. Pete became my business manager when I was hospitalized, learned the mystery coding system on the monthly bills. He scrutinized each one, asked me about medications and treatment, questioned dubious items. Frequently he found overcharges that took him to the billing department for correction. The computer number for the disposable catheter the nurses used four times a day was one digit different from an indwelling Foley catheter, but the price difference was five dollars compared to twenty-five for the Foley. Mistakes were unintentional, but the corrections made possible more days of hospital care.

The third week of March I backed my wheelchair into Doctor Richard's office. "I'll have to go home. My insurance is used up the end of this month."

"You're not finished with therapy yet. We'll have you come in as an outpatient three days a week."

"Yes," I agreed. "And I'll find a bed someplace in this hospital to rest over noontime." How could I work in therapy all morning without a short noon nap to recharge my battery for the afternoon workout?

More adjustment for the family in my full-time care. How would it be to live at home? Weekends when Pete was there to care for me were easy—but every day? For five and a half months I had lived within the protective womb of the hospital. Nurses came when I rang, washed and dressed me, moved me from wheelchair to bed and back again. Could I live with a family where people had their own interests? Could they care for me? The more I thought about it, the more apprehensive I became.

Time tromped toward April.

17
Home

Home to stay. I felt as wobbly-legged and insecure as the day Joe pulled me to my feet after my accident and told me to take the first step. The prospect of life permanently out of the hospital womb, away from nursing care, appeared as cold, hard and unpredictable as the floor had looked those first shaking moments.

Life at 561 West Main Street adapted for my needs. Pete had installed a second stair-railing so I could grasp one in each hand as I went upstairs to bed. Each evening I ascended with Pete behind me, should I lose my balance. In the morning I descended one riser to sit on the top step before bumping down the rest of the stairs, one carpeted plank at a time, on my bottom. Months passed before the long incline ceased to look like a parachute-less free fall, and I could walk down the thirteen treads.

Changes began in January during my first weekend home from City Rehabilitation Hospital. An ancient oak bedside commode that had belonged to my great-grandmother (I descended from generations of attic hoarders) made the three or four nighttime excursions easier.

Each morning Pete catheterized me from a supply of sterile packs. He tugged slacks over my hips, slid on a blouse, shoes and socks before I descended the stairs to a wheelchair borrowed from New

Holland's American Legion. They generously supplied the town with crutches, walkers and wheelchairs on a donation basis.

On the four days a week I now spent at home, Pete stayed around the house or ran short errands between my trips to the bathroom. He made us toast or cereal for breakfast and fat ham and cheese or tomato and lettuce sandwiches for lunch. At three o'clock Pete's mother came to prepare supper and discuss the next day's menu. Oma insisted that it was my house and I was the boss.

During the day I backed my wheelchair through the house to answer the telephone, load plates and flatwear on my lap to set the table, watch television or entertain visitors.

Pete set posts in the ground under the walnut tree behind the garage, fastened stair-railings to them and constructed twenty-eight feet of parallel bars. April softened the days. Every clear day Pete hoisted me to my feet, and I practiced walking. The laps increased and the grass between the rails wore to a rut as the walnut, persimmon and elms budded, then leafed and colored to fall's amber and mahogany. While I walked, Lady Dog sniffed the hazelnut bushes or chased squirrels into the chestnut trees. The neighbors came out to talk. It was good to see old friends but I was uncomfortable, felt like society's fallen crumb, sensitively aware that while I was once a doctor in the community, now I could not stand tall.

Was it purely pride, foolish pride? Perhaps, after months of bed and wheelchair, weeks of submitting to care by others, I still had a mind set against being handicapped. I had not overcome abhorrence to disability. Stroke patients recovered their ability to walk by leaning on four-footed quad canes as they limped around the gym, often one arm hanging in a sling. My sympathy for them burned so deep that I did not want to touch the embers of pain, did not want to be counted with them as they too bent over to watchdog the movements of each step across the floor.

A regular cane was too unstable for my tottering balance. In June Joe took away my Canadian crutches and placed a quad cane in my right hand. I crossed the gym after several uncertain tries. It was a great triumph, but the quad cane gave me a crippled pathetic feeling. A friend wrote about a cane with a large plunger-like foot. I searched out and bought one. It was clumsy and unusual, but it stood by itself and was not a quad cane. I practiced with the cane only in therapy.

Without crutches or someone holding the top of my slacks, I felt like a tower seesawing without guy wires, about to crash, until Craig tricked me. He followed at my heels as we started across the gym. A minute later he stood ten feet before me, his boyish face grinning gleefully. The walk had been solo. Concentrating as always on my feet, I had not heard him run behind a partition to face me. "Here I am." He laughed.

The cane became my companion. Finally I had a free hand for carrying a pocketbook, but that divided my concentration between walking and maintaining a grasp with the left hand. "I carried an envelope home today," I bragged to Doctor Richard. "Didn't drop it." It was a marvelous feat. I worried about the inevitable day when I would let my cane fall. I had never picked anything from the floor, worried that leaning so far would unbalance me.

"I dropped my cane yesterday," I boasted to Craig. Picking it up had been as wonderful as the first time, months before, when I had conquered paging the great leaves of the Sunday paper.

"Then what?" Therapists Joe and Craig shared my victories.

"Picked it up by myself," I said, remembering how gingerly I had bent from the waist, slow and stiff as a rusted hinge, fingers extended to fumble the cane into grasp. With as much care I had stood erect again.

***

With warming Pennsylvania weather came spring fever. In all our New Holland years, not one season had passed where I was not behind the rototiller as soon as the drying soil could be aroused without producing curdled clods. I lost the annual battle with weeds, but when my freezers filled by September, the victory was mine.

Disability does not hammer down desire. May's warm sunny days churned the earth-blood in this farmer's veins. I could not get out of the wheelchair by myself, let alone think of stirring up last year's stalks and weeds.

Now Pete, who had tilled the rose bed but set his size thirteens firmly against collaborating with peas, carrots or onions, except on his plate, made his ultimate personal sacrifice. He offered to plant a vegetable garden in the plot of last year's skeletal vines if I would supervise. I sopped up sunshine while my husband turned the ground, then dropped peas, carrot and spinach seeds, plus cabbage, broccoli and lettuce plants. That summer I hand weeded from the wheelchair while Pete hacked with a hoe. Nothing inside the house could replace the damp odor, the satisfying grainy feel of fresh earth between my fingers, as I pulled lamb's-quarters and crab grass along rows of beans on the days I did not go to therapy at the hospital.

On the three hospital days each week, we arose early so Pete could catheterize, dress, breakfast and deposit me by wheelchair at physiotherapy. After time in the gym with therapist Joe or Craig, I lunched in the cafeteria. Nurses, medical staff or employee friends took my tray through the line and found a space for my wheelchair at their table.

Old friend, generous Barbara, nursing supervisor of the obstetrical department, took me to the lavatory after lunch and found an empty bed. She covered it with a sheet blanket for my short nap before time to go to Occupational Therapy. Barb returned me to the wheelchair, and I wheeled away to stack cones, increase the strength of my wrist and improve finger function by pulling them against the force of rubber bands. Another hour in physiotherapy before Pete came to return me to New Holland. Enroute we discussed plans for our trip to Arizona.

After Pete sold Spring Gulch Campground, he began planning a move to Arizona, claiming that the warmer climate would ease the aches in his injured leg. I licked my finger and held it to the wind. It blew toward the Southwest. The velocity was increasing. Previously absorbed and busy in my medical practice, the move had not interested me. I preferred to think of living in Arizona in the far distant future. Not my husband. After searching through the state, he had invested in a taxi business in Scottsdale. At intervals he flew to consult with his manager. Mid-April was his next trip.

I would go with him, take Barbara with us. Barbara had helped Pete decipher my monthly bills, been my nurse in the ambulance when I was transported to City Rehabilitation, improved my comfort daily in a multitude of ways. She was unmarried and could arrange time off. Barbara and Pete looked forward to the trip.

Only two weeks out of the hospital and traveling in a wheelchair, my dependency on others gave me a bottomless apprehension. How could we manage in the small toilet of an airplane? Even with help I was not steady enough to walk down an aisle in-flight. Could we make the long trip through the Chicago terminal in time to catch our connecting flight? All unfounded fears. We checked my wheelchair as baggage. The airlines provided a wheelchair and someone to push it from curb to plane door. On the tarmac at Harrisburg Airport two attendants strapped me to a narrow chair, carried me up the steps into the plane and to my seat. In Chicago and Phoenix a wheelchair and attendant met the 737 in the jetway, pushed me to the baggage claim area, then the curb.

Mornings at Scottsdale I waited in bed until Pete or Barb dressed me and pattern-exercised my arms and legs as Joe had instructed. I cannot say if patterning had any long-term effect, but it did improve my walking for an immediate period. The remainder of the day Barb pushed my wheelchair as we browsed Scottsdale's fascinating shops or took drives into the desert.

When Pete toured with us, I rode on the back seat where I could stretch out my stiff legs. As the car sped past cacti and paloverde, I flexed my hands against the resistance of a rubber-banded exerciser; squeeze-release, squeeze-release, until both hands demanded rest. My goal was to clench them, to touch finger tips against the palms by the time I left Arizona for our next stop in Colorado to visit our daughters.

In Denver we also stopped to see my former roommate, Cindy, at Craig Hospital for the spinal-cord-injured. Cindy had transferred there from City Rehabilitation. Barb and I were amazed and fascinated to see the adaptive aids and computer appliances making life easier and more independent for quadriplegics. They even danced and played ball in wheelchairs. I left Craig Hospital relieved that when fully recovered, a wheelchair, Canadian crutches or adaptive aids would not be a part of my life. My hands were becoming more useful and I could contract them into a fist. Rising out of a chair was my next goal.

I yearned more than ever for the day I could rise unassisted from the wheelchair, to transfer from bed to chair alone, to stand up whenever I wished. Doubts, like the first wisps of clouds on the horizon before a rainstorm, were beginning to form. I brushed them away, still believed that within the next five months all my disabilities would be overcome, and I would return to full practice again. It had been promised six months ago.

Back in therapy Joe and Craig concentrated their skills on teaching me to rise from the seated position. Not every milepost was easily passed. Craig exercised and strengthened my legs by attaching rubber tubing to the rowing machine. My legs seemed more than strong enough to push my body up, but I could not coordinate the procedure. "Throw yourself forward from the chair," Joe insisted. The tile floor looked hard. I feared falling face down. "I'll catch you. I won't let you bounce more than twice." All the grunting, thrusting and pushing failed. My bottom seemed too heavy.

The last week in July I finally accomplished it in Occupational Therapy. With a table before me I stretched to reach a cone. By bending forward, then pressing hard against the locked wheelchair with both legs while pushing up with my hands against the chair arms, I gradually stood. "I did it. I stood up without help," I shouted. The occupational therapists called Joe from the gym next door. With concentration and effort I repeated the rise in slow motion. Now everything would be different, the world bigger, the world mine. Coming and going would be mine to control. There would be no limits to progress. A great victory, the second one that month.

The first had been during July's third week. I wheeled triumphantly into therapy to announce, "Guess what? I dressed myself this morning. All Pete did was tie my shoes." Sitting on the edge of the bed, I had pulled on elastic-banded underwear and slacks. Lying on the bed, I wiggled them over my hips, losing hand grips several times. Getting into a brassiere unassisted was a concern. First I ordered one that hooked in the front, but generosity in that part of my anatomy made stuffing and closing more than I could manage. Then I recalled fun bets among nurses about whether more women closed their bras by reaching behind their back to hook them or snagged them in front and slid them around. Problem solved, seizing both ends in front, elastic snapping from my awkward hands several times, I maneuvered the hook-and-rotate step before wrestling and wiggling the straps over both shoulders. Blouses or sweaters were all "over the head, no buttons or back-closing zipper" style. Capturing a foot to battle a stubborn sock over it was the next feat to be conquered. My stiff legs did not want to bend enough to bring the toes within reach. After several tries I bagged them and finished the job.

Successful dressing is ruled by choice of clothing. Back zippers are allowed now, but no buttons where I cannot see to direct fingers that slide away with a will, direction and life of their own. No side closings where I cannot watch a left hand with no sense of where it is in space (loss of proprioception). A solo game I play is moving the left hand under the bed covers then guessing where it lies. If I think abdomen, I find it stretched by my side, or if I believe it beside me, I find it resting on my left leg. When slicing anything in the kitchen, the position of my hand becomes crucial. Pete often clips a left earring into place. Small blouse buttons are an aggravation. Fingers slow in tying shoes prefer granny bows to square knots. But I dress and undress every day. I do it myself!

It had to be difficult, a strain for the family to watch me struggle with the effort of daily routine. Sometimes I slapped at Pete's hands if he wanted to pick something from the floor that I had dropped. He became angry at my "me do" attitude. My husband wanted to help me but I became irritated, wanted to do things without assistance and wanted no impatience on his part or lack of belief that I could do it. Other times he said, "Do it yourself," and walked away. When we had an angry confrontation, I became more determined to be independent and my abilities improved through rude stubbornness. I suffered unnecessary assistance from strangers, but wondered how I could recover if people insisted on doing even little things for me.

Recovery was the word inscribed on my mind like a billboard. Able to get out of any chair firm enough to push against as I rose, I determined to drive the car. The prospect of maneuvering so much power was awesome. What if it was too much for me? What if I lost control, hit someone, had a flat tire along the road? I had to try, had to find out if I could do it.

Mid-August, a Sunday afternoon when the big parking lot at the shopping center east of town was empty, Pete parked in its middle. "Let's see what you can do," he said, turning off the engine.

I slid behind the wheel of my Pacer station wagon, a familiar and comfortable feeling. My fingers were too weak to turn the key in the ignition. A great start. By bracing the stiff wire key ring against the key, I pulled toward the floor, levering it like a handle, until the engine turned over. The only other obstacles were the lamp standards. No problem. Of all my goals, of all the markers I had passed, driving the car was the only skill that did not need to be relearned. My right leg responded to brake and gas by reflex action. The Pacer moved victoriously around and around the big lot, then out onto the street toward home, slowly, carefully and as tensely as an overstretched slingshot. I tilted the steering wheel far forward to stretch my stiff arms. Only the right one controlled the wheel. The weak left one moved the turn signal.

I could now drive myself to physiotherapy sessions! Parking near the entrance, I slid my feet to the ground, pushed both calves against the car and became upright. Walking with slow deliberate steps, avoiding a curb, I skirted wide around an open stairwell and hugged the building. Pete was not there to catch or balance me. If I lost my balance, the wall was close. Often my elbows were skinned raw and scabbed from rubbing against the rough bricks as I passed. If I fell, getting up without help was impossible. Vulnerability begets fear. Each hospital trip I walked slowly, with deliberate care. I never fell.

Some moments in life are sculpted on our minds like letters engraved on a monument. How long the aisle in our country church had seemed as I clung to Father's arm before the wedding march began. How I wished Mother had stitched the hem of my gown two inches shorter as I tripped toward the altar. A bomb might as well have landed in the church yard the Sunday we emerged from services to learn about the disastrous attack on Pearl Harbor. Later as an inner race groove grinder during the war, I remember standing in the lunch line at SKF Ballbearing Plant as the cafeteria loudspeaker blared the A-bomb drop on Japan. Never forgotten during a frigid January inauguration, the memorable words, "ask not what your country can do for you," as they beat like a drum from our black and white TV. At that inauguration I watched poet laureate, Robert Frost, stand white-haired in the cold breezes as the pages of his poem drifted away in the wind. As if only yesterday, I pushed a dime into a parking meter on Ephrata's Main Street and overheard a man on the sidewalk say, "Shot during a parade in Dallas. Don't know if he's alive."

It was like that with the inevitable truth that I would never return to my office. During gait training. Walking exercise time. The month of August. I walked two tiles into the hall beyond the gym door, my left foot stepping forward. Joe, close behind me, verbalized the truth which had lain beneath the sea of recovery, a muddy wreck of suspicion, a reality I had not wanted to eyeball. "Your progress has been good," he said. "You will continue to improve. No one can say how much. You won't be the same as before the accident."

I held my breath, stunned, waiting for Joe's next prediction. "You will be able to get around by yourself," he continued, his voice quiet, as calm and factual as if he had told me that rain was forecast. "Your hands will be able to do most things, maybe not sew fine stitches."

"Oh." I answered with the same matter-of-fact professional voice. Who cared about mending or dressmaking? I hated any kind of sewing except the thrust of a needle and the knotting of thread at a perineal repair after the delivery of a baby

We continued down the hall. The mud had washed away. The wreck was my medical practice—standing at the delivery table encouraging a woman, the pulse beat of a fetal monitor, the flush of excitement on hearing a newborn cry, the baby's slippery warm body on my arm. There would be no more night calls in winter storms and summer heat, familiar trusting faces across my desk.

For most of a year I had put my future on hold, letting the world glide by, imagining that I sat on a limb above everything, watching but not participating. In psychology class we had learned that it was mentally unhealthful for a person to observe the world as an outsider. It was time, necessary now, for me to slide out of the tree and back into life. But when my feet attempted to touch solid ground, the world had kept moving; it was not the same place I had left. I had expected to resume life at home and office without losing a step. Never in my wildest dreams was there a vision of the future with limitations, a cane to walk, the years ahead without stethoscope and black bag. Retirement was not supposed to begin now but when I decided, at my control, after gradual reduction of patients and responsibilities, years ahead. This was too soon. Rocking on the porch, cuddling grandchildren, driving to visit old friends better fit my plans for retirement. I felt like a new mother who expected to birth a perfect infant and was told that her baby had a deformity. What I had perceived as a mere detour in life, a bypass that would return to the main route, had become the permanent road, the only one. Surely incomplete recovery should have been the prognosis as early as the night I fell in the camping trailer.

"Why didn't you tell me the truth, that my medical practice was over the night of my accident?" I asked the neurosurgeon who had attended me in the emergency room. We met in the hall one day. During his numerous hospital visits I came to know him as friendly and concerned.

"I had never met you. I didn't know how you would react," he said. "Maybe you would have given up without trying."

His explanation was medically justified, but I have always felt cheated, lied to, concerning *my* life. Would things have been different? I also pondered if anything would have changed if the psychologist at City Rehabilitation had delved into my reason for believing that I did not need help in adapting to life as a person disabled.

The word DISABLED burned like a fresh brand; this scar would belong to me forever for everyone to see. There had been tears, frustrations, disappointments, low periods in my recovery, but through everything I had held to the vision of total healing. Running in my dreams first slowed to walking, then locomotion disappeared, and I no longer moved on my feet when asleep. I wanted to know that the nightmare was over, but now both feet touched the ground and this was forever.

I slipped into a depression hidden from family and friends. Joe had told me that a percentage of spinal cord patients resort to suicide. I resolved never to allow this although the thought came frequently. There must be good days ahead, some cause for which to live. A strong feeling of purpose had confined me within the walls of college for eight years. The pull of destiny helped me through internship and the struggle of early practice years. What now? The children were grown and did not need me. I could not return to my office as it had been, and too many years had elapsed since general practice days. My ego kept whispering that life was not over, that there was something for me to accomplish.

In September a friend died in an accident. Why did the able-bodied die while I was left with wheelchair and cane? Alone in the kitchen, I laid my head against the counter top. My wedding and engagement rings, now returned to my finger, stabbed my forehead. Tears dropped onto my lap as I wished that fate had taken me. A row of evil knives dangled in a rack near my head. My resolve held firm.

If destiny had served a good purpose before, I should trust it now, but this blanket of self-pity seemed too heavy to shake off. I wondered why sadness insisted on shadowing me.

Then, as if an unseen hand pointed the way on a map, my eyes opened and I remembered a maternal infant-bonding seminar years earlier at the Bond Hotel in Cleveland. It had been a wonderful and diverse congregation of doctors, nurses, midwives, long-haired commune members and mothers sitting lotus-limbed in hallways nursing babies. One session dealt with the loss of body parts such as an arm, leg or breast and the resulting grief.

Remembering the seminar, I raised my head from the counter in disbelief and recognition. Grief! Me? Yes! Grief for a lost yesterday, a second Thanksgiving without independent walking and soon Christmas without running. The running I had predicted by my first hospital Christmas was impossible. I was in mourning.

In retrospect I recognized Elizabeth Kübler-Ross's stages of grief. First, shock and numbness, followed by denial. Being a physician, I should have had insight into my prognosis. Was my consistent belief that I would return to my office in a year actually denial?

Anger is the second stage; anger because plans and activities are interrupted. What could have been more interruptive than being unable to give medical attention to the many women depending on me to deliver their babies? The guilt of letting them down led to greater anger.

I envied those who could still enjoy life. Drunks and criminals walked across the TV screen during the six o'clock news, and, playing Pharisee, I resented their freedom and mobility. Was the disappointment felt at my pastor's first visit unjustified anger? The accident had been a solo performance. Only I had tangled a foot in the electric cord, and there was no one to blame, to vent anger on.

The third stage, bargaining, I resolved to omit. There are stories of soldiers in trenches, people who face death due to accident or disease, who bargain with God. Disability, not death, was at issue. I had nothing to promise God but my body and my future. He already controlled them. Feeling beaten down by my disability, I feared entering a pact.

The fourth stage is depression. In its twistings and turnings depression began within days after my accident. Its tentacles are still visible, braided with frustration and anger. Plans still crash or must be altered because of physical limitations. Food preparation and cooking are accomplishable, but I cannot carry dishes to the table. On a vacation in Bavaria I climbed a steep hill to tour Neuschwanstein Castle. Then I fell in the restroom and was carted away in an ambulance to an emergency room before I saw the wonders of King Leopold.

On television I watched a young quadriplegic request the right to end his life. Unable to move from his neck to his toes, he asked for assistance in suicide. After therapy with three psychologists, he felt there seemed no reason for him to continue living. Psychologists have been invaluable in helping the handicapped adjust to new lives. Hearsay states that if suddenly a cure were found for spinal-cord-injured patients, the estimated number of psychologists required to counsel them during their readjustment would be astronomical — more than available.

The fifth stage of grief is acceptance, during which neither depression nor anger exists. I must accept my limitations, but like the quarry slave, I do it kicking and fighting. Often the risks I take are foolish, like driving solo from Phoenix to Alabama for an Elderhostel week. Alone, I pumped gas, hunted motels and restaurants. Struggling to open a heavy door at the Montgomery college, I fell and fractured a bone in my foot, making traveling more difficult. Driving home, at a rest stop along Interstate 70, I lost my balance and seriously injured my back.

Learning to suffer the indulgence of others when for years I had been the care giver has been a bitter dose. People rush to assist the handicapped. Family members know better after my cross words or the rude swipes of my hand. From strangers I politely accept assistance, needed or not. Pity is unendurable. There is no room for it.

Steps without a railing and heavy doors are my worst problems. I frequently ask strangers to hold doors open. A lady in the Tulsa Airport held my arm to help me onto the escalator, released my arm too soon and I sprawled out as the stairway moved up to the gates. A man heard our screams and stood me up like a jointless manikin in time to walk off at the top, unhurt. The thought of what I must have looked like riding feet first up the escalator still makes me chuckle. Our son Paul who was busy checking luggage laughed too and regretted missing the event.

I was deeply self-conscious about my appearance. Acceptance came hard. It did not keep me at home. Slow paced I move along, conscious of watching my feet; it is impossible to make eye contact with people unless I stop walking. I find many pennies along a path. Acquaintances pass unnoticed.

Most difficult to reconcile are attitudes about the handicapped. People act as if we are not as mentally bright as other people or as if we are indigent. Detailed explanations about obvious matters amuse and disturb me. Strangers tend to talk over my head to my companion.

People often stuff the proverbial shoe into their mouths! One day after therapy Joe placed me in a regular seat instead of a wheelchair. The porter who transported patients from room to therapy entered the room and said, "You look normal sitting like that." During sound sleep, when I first went home, my respirations became very shallow and quiet. Pete said one morning, "You breathe so slowly at night that I have to look to be sure you're alive. Last night I couldn't see the motion and thought at last . . ." It was the only time he acknowledged my innermost desire and had blurted it out before he thought. When I went to a photographer for a passport photo, he asked, "How long are you going to be laid up like this?" A glimpse of how I appeared to others startled me because I was so proud to be able to come and go places as I wished.

Throughout recovery nothing could be done about my handicap, but the future could still be molded by choices. Control was still mine. Joe once told me that most of my progress would probably occur within the first year. Improvement would be slower after that period. "You must relearn in a year what a baby develops in several years," he said. Often I identified with my children, remembering how they had rolled about in their playpens. I also struggled on the mats or lost balance as I walked. Every day I chose to keep trying, keep walking, keep exercising. Active longevity has been a family trait, and I did not like the alternative image of a woman shawl-wrapped, seated in a wheelchair, needing help for every activity. The choice is mine. Every day!

Through it all I felt blessed. I was not confined permanently to a wheelchair. My legs were numb. The left arm and leg were still lost in space, but my brain was unaffected. The use of my hands had returned. Running was impossible but I could walk, slowly at least. I was fortunate.

***

When I lifted my head from the kitchen counter's chopping block and grasped the idea that I was in a state of mourning, I had at last something to hold in my fist. It was time to end this grief. The cure was obvious but not easy. The remedy for me was to become busy, so deeply involved outside myself that there was no time for grief. I needed a project, something to do, a goal.

The difficulty lay in breaking out of my cage. For most of a year all effort had been concentrated on recovery. Each week I yearned more to take charge of my kitchen, but Oma enjoyed her responsibilities and the daily family companionship. "You can't do it," she insisted when I pressed to get a meal. Our differences of opinion chafed until it became an open sore.

Finally, Oma needed a day off to go on a senior citizen bus tour. After many explicit instructions, I was allowed full kitchen duty for an evening. I locked the wheelchair behind me as I worked at the counter, stove or sink in case my knees buckled and I flopped backward. Supper proved not only possible but successful. Daily kitchen involvement increased. Oma went away more often.

Bread-baking became a regular duty as I exercised my arms kneading and rekneading each batch. I baked a box of loaves for the Boy Scout blue and gold banquet. When my legs collapsed, the wheelchair caught me. Each week my legs endured longer standing periods and my arms became stronger. Pete and our sons reveled in fat slices of crusty whole wheat bread slathered with butter and jam.

Not only was I not confident enough on my cane to become involved in any community work, which ceased the night I fell, but attending park board meetings or hospital functions was also not the same from a wheelchair. The winds blowing toward the Southwest were picking up. Pete was determined to trade his lawn mower and winter coat for life in warmer Phoenix, Arizona. Without a medical practice to hold me in Pennsylvania, I reluctantly agreed. We would fly west in October and hunt a new home in the desert.

18
New Beginnings

Racing blithely down the road, my eyes focused only on steering the course. I did not see the detour signs. I had had two objectives before my shingle became weatherbeaten and fell onto the grass.

First, although I had not kept a count of the numerous sets of twins I delivered, my frequently expressed desire was a set of triplets, all babies surviving.

Mary Stoltzfus's last child was several years old, and she hankered fruitlessly for a baby. Finally a bulge under her apron became obvious and larger than estimated for her stage of pregnancy. But Mary was a short woman, slender as a pump handle, with shafts of legs that ran from kitchen to garden to barn and back again. She had always looked like a distorted string bean when pregnant. At seven months I hospitalized her with leaking membranes and a suspicion of twins. Triplets confirmed. Several days later she delivered two boys; one whose middle name was Harold for the pediatrician, one the middle name of Joel for the obstetrical resident and a girl bearing Grace for a middle name. The boys spent stormy weeks on life-support systems, then incubators, but all babies were welcomed home by a happy family.

My other wish was an avoided situation, a brag. Despite many near accidents no woman had delivered a baby in my car. Amniotic fluid had been mopped off my plastic car seats leaving deposits of salt impossible to scrub away. But I boasted that despite cop chases and escorts, running country roads at full speed with high beam headlights and horn blaring through crossroads, no panting mother had ever birthed enroute to the hospital.

Not until Anna Beiler, in January of my last year of practice. She was to have her baby at home, on the edge of Lancaster City. When I saw her with irregular mild contractions, leaking amniotic fluid for two days and running a mild fever, I insisted on a hospital delivery. I would take her there immediately. My car was a small two-door Pacer station wagon. Her husband and I pillowed Anna on the back seat. Aaron sat beside me. We bumped no further than the Beiler mailbox at the end of the lane before Anna had her first hard contraction. Six miles were sixty. We flew over the macadam, shortening curves, lights on. Speed increased with the frequency of contractions and intensity of panting in the back seat. Two blocks from our destination Anna shouted, "It's comin'."

"Not yet. Pant harder," I yelled back, concentrating on turning a corner, worrying what might happen to a baby delivered in the confines of the back seat.

It came. It cried. I swung onto the hospital driveway.

Forewarned from my car telephone, attendants pushed a stretcher out as I stopped against the emergency room doors. We untangled the baby from Anna's clothing and cut its cord before whisking the wrapped squalling newborn off to the pediatrician. I delivered the placenta, homestyle in a basin, before Anna was pulled and slithered off the back seat and onto a gurney. Mother and baby went home in several days. Cleaned up, the Pacer was ready for its next wild trip.

Only in retrospect are adventures amusing. At the time, spiraling down icy hills, dusting stork feathers from a shoulder as I dashed between deliveries, flat tires along country roads were frustrating inconveniences. But it was the excitement, the tension, waking to the promises of each unborn day that I missed at unmapped retirement.

As Pete and I planned a house-hunting expedition in Arizona, his next business trip in October, I felt like a tree slowly and painfully being extracted from the ground. The soil I had sunk my roots into was Lancaster County, subtitled "Garden Spot."

In Phoenix Pete left me at a senior center to watch television, read and write letters while he made business calls. We toured five houses one day with a realtor. Accustomed to the unfenced expanse of backyard against backyard, the high-walled properties of Phoenix seemed like Alcatraz. "Walls are for privacy," Mister Salesman said. No neighbor had ever squatted on our acre or violated privacy in New Holland. Not one house shown us gave the comfortable feeling that I could call home.

"There is a place for sale by the owner, near my house," the salesman said. He looked as weary as I felt.

There it was. The only place I wanted. Through a wire fence we saw the pool, palms, orange and grapefruit trees and six varieties of cacti. The ranch-style house was surrounded by an acre of wild desert. Contrary to easterners' mistaken belief that the desert is mile after mile of sand without fauna or flora, mountains lip the horizon everywhere in Arizona. Twelve miles away from the prospective real estate the McDowell Mountains, as if they belonged to the property, played changing colors with the sun.

"We'll take this one," Pete and I agreed. "Don't let it get away from us."

"Don't you want to see the house?" the agent asked.

"Not necessary. It can't be so bad that we can't live in it or change anything we don't like."

The next morning we toured the house and set settlement for January. That afternoon we flew home to sell our New Holland house and begin the gargantuan task of honing down thirty years' accumulation of beds, sofas and kitchen knickknacks so we could begin again. What had we done?

As misgivings about moving came and went, I picked up my cane and attended meetings. The hospital medical staff met at night. Driving to the restaurant gave me no problem, but unexplainable panic grabbed me as I crossed the dimly lit parking lot, hugging a line of parked cars until I reached a railing and safety inside the lit building. After moving to Phoenix, I grabbed the kitchen counter and nearly fell over when an electrical storm blackened the house. Only after I fell in a grocery store parking lot one night and cracked a kneecap did I realize that, because of my spinal cord damage, my balance depended solely upon vision. Night walking is a problem.

A problem, also, was the whole-day auction we held in May to shrink a fourteen-room house to a six-room house in Phoenix. So many memories, struggles and happy moments. The auctioneer fingered each one as dishes, sofas, beds went to the highest bidder. Sentimentality made us keep too much. Moving day rushed toward us.

Two pieces of unfinished business remained. Since I had delivered the last baby, the final time I changed my scrub suit for street clothes, my locker in the nurses' lounge had remained unopened. Cleaning it out was a thud of earth in an open grave, the farewell. I fingered the limp lab coat with DR. KAISER embroidered on the pocket before tossing it into the soiled linen hamper. Like a handful of flowers, my splattered white clogs went home to gather dust in the back of a closet. The funeral was over.

I walked everywhere with a cane, but at home it was quicker and easier to back the wheelchair forty-five feet through the living room into the kitchen. The chair was like a baby's pacifier clung to beyond necessity. The week before we left New Holland, I surrendered it to its lender.

The entire nation burned under the fiery thumb of an endless and record-breaking heat spell the July seventh morning we left Country Squire Motel in New Holland to walk through our house on Main Street one last time. Our echoing footsteps in the vacant rooms drummed discordant accusing beats. We spoke little. Pete, Oma, Lady Dog and I climbed into my Pacer and took the road west.

The little station wagon dragged behind it a ton of U-Haul trailer containing odd-shaped and extra items that would not fit into the full moving truck. We traveled no further than the mountains of Pennsylvania before realizing that using the air conditioner overheated the engine. The humidity is aquatic in the eastern states during July. People gasp for breath like fish. In Ohio Lady, riding behind the back seat in the sun, was the first to rebel. Enough was enough. The dog bounded over Oma onto my lap. I did not need a yellow Labrador fur piece. No coaxing, shouting or shoving could move her. In Indiana we bought white contact paper to cover the expanse of glass behind us and Lady returned to her place.

Pete mopped his face and leaned forward to cool his back. The heat turned Oma's face red. Lunching in a park the second day, I flung myself onto the grass and poured ice water over my neck and down my back in a panicked effort to cool off. Riding the long steep rolls of western roads, nothing but blasts of furnaced air swept through the open car windows. We stopped in McLean, Texas for an afternoon drink and to enjoy a few minutes of air conditioning. Everywhere people talked about deaths due to the extreme heat. I felt as if I would explode. Pete put cold towels to my neck. "Get me an ambulance," I said, half-conscious. An hour or so in a cold emergency room, cold compresses and an intravenous infusion cooled me down. Later I learned that spinal-cord-injured patients are more susceptible to heat prostration.

The third day we traveled through cooler New Mexico mountains and arrived in Phoenix at night. The moving truck, backed into the dry wash before our new home, had beaten us. The next day we unloaded in 115 degree heat. Again I wondered, what had we done? Would it ever get cold in Arizona?

Cold is as intolerable as heat for me. I am a snake in a snowbank and do not realize that I am cold until I cannot move and my fingers need to be pried open. One October we spent a day traveling beautiful Canyon de Chelly with ancient dwellings under the brows of patina-streaked cliffs. Although the northern Arizona sun reflected off colorful wind-sculpted formations, layers of blankets bundled and tucked did nothing to warm us. By mid-afternoon I was as stiff as a corpse. The guide allowed me to ride with him in the heated cab of the open truck. All afternoon I thought of returning to the motel and soaking in a hot tub. I imagined the wonderful flush of heat as I sank into the water. Disappointment! I forgot my loss of sensation. Until immersed to my shoulders, there was no comforting satisfaction, but the warming made me relaxed and happy.

Happiness did not rule every day in Arizona. We knew no neighbors and had no close friends. I brought out the new sewing machine I purchased before leaving New Holland. The first item I mended was the brassiere cut from me the night of my accident by a nurse in the emergency room. Zigzagging over and over left a thick scar but it was stronger than before. I sewed several summer blouses and slacks but soon learned that I did not like the seamstress trade any better than when Grandmother bossed my pinning and ripping as a teenager.

It takes time and work to fit into a new community. Pete had business associates. I found a church and attended a women's circle. The Heard Museum, concerned with Indian art and artifacts, offered the opportunity to take a guide course which taught much about the Southwest and admitted me to a valued circle of friends. I needed more.

In the fall Pete fenced in a plot of ground and ran irrigation lines for a vegetable garden. I contacted the state agricultural division, read the gardening section of the paper and learned when and what flowers and vegetables to plant in our new Arizona climate.

Life was busy but there was still something missing. Hoeing grass from broccoli and cauliflower, dusting the house were not enough. A writing career still pooled in the back of my mind. There were stories to be told if I had the skill to write them.

February 1980, before we moved, I had attended a one-day writers' seminar at The People's Place in Intercourse, Pennsylvania. Author Katie Funk Wiebe stood before us and told of her beginnings, how only a few years earlier she could not have imagined speaking before a group of writers. "Not me," I whispered under my breath. "I'll never stand up there." March 1987, after *Dr. Frau* my first book was published, I stood there.

After two weeks of Dorothy Lykes's writing class at Scottsdale Senior Center, I bought an inexpensive electric typewriter at K Mart. My writing career was born. Like any newborn, it cried a lot and needed frequent feedings. Dorothy was a doting mother. The next semester she helped me enroll in the first of many creative writing classes at Arizona State University. My first homework contained all the "do nots" of writing. The carnivorous professor had a feast.

I read articles and books about my new career, saw the same intense hopeful faces at every seminar, heard the same advice sliced and mauled over and over until truths emerged like old tree roots breaching the earth. This adolescent writer rebelled. Seminars, reading, college were of no benefit unless I put pen to the paper, corrected my sins without shame, wrote and rewrote seventy times seven.

I have watched writing aspirants flounder in ink like sparrows splashing in a puddle. It feels good, but some feathers never become wet. For me getting a little wet seemed better than never jumping in.

My involvement in writing became deeper, but I still mourned my physical losses.

Five years into my detour, I explained to a friend how I felt about needing to watch each footstep, my faltering pace, the frustrations of limited activities particularly at night. "I am like a great stump in a forest after the ravaging fire has passed," I said. "Burning embers still smolder deep at the roots, ready to break out again, but now I am too busy to look over the charred edges." Returning to college was my best move.

The university campus is designed for access to the handicapped; each building is ramped and has electrically operated doors. Wheelchairs of quadriplegics, paraplegics and other disabilities are everywhere. Seated on a bench, I watched them wheel past and wondered how they felt beneath their facades. What were the private thoughts and desires behind the young faces? How did they get through a day?

"Working students come to my room each morning to dress me and get me ready for the day," a young classmate, chair-bound since birth, told me. "Another helper puts me to bed at night. I pay five dollars in the middle of the day for someone to take me to the toilet. I could write a book about toilets."

This subject among handicapped people brings head-shaking and sarcastic grins. Each one offers a book of experiences. Pete and I could not go out to a public place when he had to stand-pivot me in a restroom. One afternoon at an Arizona park above the Mogollon Rim I could not rise from a low pit toilet seat. In my struggles I caught my arm behind the assist bar. Worried about a fracture, I yelled for Pete. The woman in the next open stall hugged her jeans around her hips as my husband came dashing around the barrier. Most restroom doors displaying the handicapped insignia are too heavy for me to open. Risking black suspicious stares, Pete frequently pushes them for me. Restaurant restrooms are often up or down steep steps and along twilit hallways. My secret fear is to descend onto a hopper too low to rise from. How long before I would be missed, before someone came along? What a fate. Restrooms along interstates are usually well planned except the flush mechanism which is either inaccessibly embedded in the wall or too stiff for my fingers to operate.

On my April Arizona trip with Barbara, who alone fills an airplane toilet space, she took advantage of ground time to help me to the lavatory. The absurd stewardess insisted on latching the door. Unable to get up or down by myself, I pressed my tummy against Barbara, who could scarcely fumble my slacks from her skirt while we took turns breathing.

In one restaurant Barbara heaved her weight against an unused jukebox to push my wheelchair past the obstruction to the handicap restroom. At a national park listing handicapped facilities, the barrier was so close to the entrance that Barbara had to stand me against the wall while she folded the wheelchair enough to enter the washroom, then reseat me.

I was on a walker after a hip replacement when I flew home to Lancaster County to promote *Dr. Frau*. I wrote *Dr. Frau* because I wanted to preserve in ink how I saw things. I wanted to tell the world that although the Plain People dress differently, they have the same basic pleasures and interests as folks everywhere. I wanted my Amish and Mennonite friends to read the stories and laugh with me. They did. Letters came, guessing the identity of characters in the stories.

People came to a reception held in New Holland's fire hall on a rainy night. On another evening the firehouse in Intercourse was shadowed with black hats and shawls waiting thirty minutes for the doors to open. Friends of the New Holland library sponsored an evening at the Lutheran Church of greeting and book-signing. I wanted to talk over old times with each family, but the crush of time and people barely offered an opportunity for a greeting. It was not only the women seen through pregnancy and delivery whom I remembered with rosy thoughts, but also their husbands who had toasted me with homemade root beer, shared cookies at midnight or opened cans of pretzels and chips while their wives paced and panted. My love of fresh bread spread with peanut butter, amber molasses dripping off crisp crusts, came from waiting a night with Joe Stoltzfus.

John and Sara Weaver lined up to shake my hand. John called me too late to take his wife to the hospital for a breech delivery, their ninth baby. "Wait a minute," John said when Sara and her newborn rested comfortably in bed. "You deserve something extra tonight." I waited with curiosity as John took a flashlight to the cellar. Minutes later he reappeared with two glasses of amber liquid. That applejack wore fingers of golden satin as it slid across my tongue. John told me how he made his nectar with apple juice, raisins and brown sugar.

At the Intercourse reception, Eli King stood with the men against a back wall of the firehouse. I will never forget Eli, how he started my car at one o'clock in the morning. It took no special intelligence to understand that tired whirr as I turned the key in the ignition.

I looked up the slate walk to the old brick farmhouse where I had slumped four hours on a hard chair in the Amish kitchen waiting for Lizzie to birth number four. Eli would have to help me.

My flashlight beam guided me back through the cold washhouse, past the great iron kettle that heated Monday's wash water, past a table of half-consumed pies, bowls of leftover food and empty canning jars. I gave a warning knock and stepped into Kings' kitchen.

Eli, stocking-footed as he had been all evening, stretched a hand toward the stair door. "I was just going to bed," he said. "Time to get up for milkin' in four hours. What brought you back so soon?" He squinted at me. The dull light of a lamp on the kitchen counter sank his brown eyes deep under a broad brow and spread his straggly beard into the shadows.

"I'll need help to get my car moving. Battery's dead."

Eli's mother stopped mid-kitchen. "When I came home from daughter Anna's last night at ten, your inside car lights were on." She walked toward the bedroom beside the kitchen with hot tea for Lizzie. "I thought you knew about it."

"No," I said. "That would do it. I was in a rush when Eli told me to hurry over here. Guess I didn't close the door right."

Eli laced up work shoes. He took an old coat from a hook behind the black space heater and clapped a tattered broad-brimmed hat on his head before going to the barn. I heard his soft voice speak gently to the horses as he drove them from the stable to my car.

Eli slid under the bumper. His coat grated gravel and ruts at the edge of the barnyard. "I'll find a place to hook on," he called from deep under the front end of my station wagon. Looping a chain over the frame, he crawled out and snapped the other end to the double-tree behind the horses. Eli leaned into the open car window, his breath a wispy cloud in the March air. "Couple hundred feet you'll be through that pasture gate. Soft there. Even this team can't pull you outa that muck." He slapped leather reins against the shaggy brown backs. "Get up Joe. Go Bud."

The Chevy moved, picked up speed. I let the clutch out. The engine sputtered stinking explosions, coughed, smoked, died halfway to the pasture. Again the horses leaned into the traces. I rolled forward, let the team get to the gate. Clutch out. The engine roared and held.

"Okay," I yelled to Eli, slithering after his chain. "Thank you," I repeated as he drove Joe and Bud into the stable.

I drove home, humbled that all the gas-driven horses under my hood had been helpless without two oats-eating ones.

At the receptions I greeted friends with humility and pleasure. They lined up to shake hands, exchange a few words. Mary Weaver handed me a sack of fresh raisin cookies, Eva Horst a dozen tollhouse. Grace Stauffer brought apple snitz. "Just took them off the drying racks today," she said.

Taking the plastic bag of preserved sweet apples still warm from her hands, I fingered savored memories.

Epilogue

Trouble sneaked in like a cat burglar during the summer of 1989. It began with pain down the right leg into the big toe. A little sciatica, I thought, and waited for it to disappear. In October I flew east and blamed my poor balance on an injured foot and on neglecting to visit the gym regularly for exercise. But when I returned to Phoenix, gym exercise aggravated the growing weakness in my arms and legs. Nighttime spasms returned. I had painful cramps in the right forearm which I believed were due to sleeping with the arm flexed against my chest.

Could I possibly lose everything I had gained the last eleven years? Rapidly, my arms and legs grew weaker. As I wrote *Detour*, rejoicing in my recovery, I wondered if I would have the motivation and energy to repeat physiotherapy with its slow gains and muscular agonies.

By Thanksgiving I fell easily. Next, I could not reach the top cupboard shelves, then the lowest ones. Pete had to set items I needed on the counter where I could reach them. Surely the next day would be better. It was not. I had stepped back in time to rehabilitation and the days of therapy. Physiotherapy; that would mend my problems. I would visit the physiatrist, whom I had not seen for several years. Mid-December I entered his office using a walker, my hands contracted and stiff.

Two days later MRI (magnetic resonance imaging) in an X ray facility revealed pressure on the spinal cord in the neck area due to arthritis and four intervertebral disk herniations.

Before Christmas the final rewrite of *Detour* was tedious, my arms struggled to reach the keyboard level of my word processor, my fingers barely able to peck out letters. Pete and I flew to Tulsa to spend the holiday week with Lorelei and her family. Unable to rise from a low seat, hands uncoordinated, I could not help. I was a guest. As I huddled by the yuletide fire or wandered clumsily through the house, I remembered the same kind of Christmas eleven years before.

Returning to Phoenix, I kept my appointment with a neurosurgeon, understanding too well the surgical procedure and his grim warnings about the reaming removal of the offending disks. "With all spinal cord fibers descending the spinal canal through the neck, any area below it could be permanently affected," he said. "And you could come out of surgery a quadriplegic."

Put into words, surgery sounded even more ominous than when I had visualized it. Any slip of the drill as it ground toward the spinal canal could cause instant irreparable damage.

The surgeon continued, "I can use the posterior approach to the cervical disks, but I prefer to enter through the front of the neck. I get far better results with an anterior incision. There is the possibility of permanent voice loss since we work so close to the larynx. You could end up with a large scar on the neck."

I had anticipated danger to the spinal cord. But being unable to speak! Pete and I looked at each other. "Without surgery I will soon be a quad," I said. The doctor nodded. The decision was not easy, but I had made it even before seeing the neurosurgeon. If surgery went well, a neck scar would be insignificant.

The future was like stepping into a great void. Often as I watched paratroopers on television step into space from high above the ground, I had wondered how they felt at their first jumps. As the earth hurdled toward them, were they breathless with fear? Did they worry about their chutes jamming? Did the thought of landing terrorize them? All I saw was a graceful string of parachutes drifting earthward in a lacy tail, like a line of dandelion seeds fleeing before a puff of breath. Could I step into vacant air? What would the landing be like? The plane I rode was in a tailspin. Crashing was certain.

"There isn't much choice. The sooner we can schedule surgery, the better," I told the doctor. The earth reeled toward me. Time to jump. "I hope I can regain lost ground, use my word processor again."

"You may have to make other arrangements." He gave no promises.

Surgery was scheduled for the following Wednesday. I went home to package my life. Tie it up in case I did not survive. Laboriously I inventoried the family antiques so my daughters would know from where they came and to whom they should go. I sent both girls a copy of our family history and wished I had put other genealogies on the computer. I telephoned friends, emptied the refrigerator and packed my bag for a long absence.

I entered Phoenix's Barrow Neurological Institute. The X ray department was generous in showing me my myelogram film. I saw nearly complete occlusion of the spinal canal and knew that surgery was the right decision.

Some people do peculiar things as they come out of anesthesia. After nearly nine hours I awoke in the recovery room. I tested my voice, not by speaking, but by giving a feeble rooster crow, a game I often played with my grandchildren. The sound bleeped out; audible, weak and husky, if not identifiable. No neighboring cock answered. Within days I could speak without sounding like a bullfrog. My voice seemed normal until I attended church. The first stanza, first hymn quacked out like a mallard at mating season. I looked around to see if anyone noticed, wondered if I should continue and hope for improvement or stop singing and mouth the words.

Fresh from surgery, my hands were swollen. The painful forearm contractions were gone, my fingers relaxed and unclawed. No pains shot into my foot. I had a Foley catheter. Wonderful. I was alive and could move everything.

Several days later the resident in neurosurgery explained the marvels of the high speed drills used in the microdiskectomy. "In learning we practice on an egg," he said. "Grind off the shell, leaving the membrane." I remembered the occasional soft-shelled egg found in Father's henhouse, its pliable white membrane which punctured easily. Carrying it into the house unbroken had been a feat of gentleness.

"Can the problem of ruptured cervical disks recur?" I asked the surgeon. "How long will I be in the hospital?"

"No," he answered. "They cannot recur. You may be discharged to rehabilitation on your fourth day."

I spent the next month at Good Samaritan Rehabilitation Hospital. Every muscle was weak. I found it impossible to rise from a seated position. At first nurses dressed me. My arms were feeble and limited in function. The agonies of twice-a-day therapy returned. I remembered Community Hospital. The slogans "no pain, no gain" and "anything physical is therapy" still applied. I requested no visitors so that I could rest after therapy sessions. The hospital wheelchair van took patients to shopping malls, out to dinner, to therapy swimming. These outings integrated us into the community, made us aware of the hazards of steps, doors or barriers and educated us to plan trips. I took advantage of this training as well as the games and entertainment in the lounge. The more time I spent out of bed the stronger I became. Evening television is a sinister tempter.

If temptation for self-pity raised its scrawny head, it was only necessary for me to look around the gym and watch other patients at therapy. Amputees practiced walking on combative stumps. Patients requiring oxygen carried tanks and tubing with them as they practiced walking or strengthened their arms. Quadriplegics, married to their wheelchairs, learned to adapt to the non-handicapped world. In several weeks I could dress myself and had shed the wheelchair for a walker.

After four weeks I left the hospital to continue therapy as an outpatient. I still have much to accomplish by retraining weak muscles. Using my word processor is not as easy as it was six months ago, but it is possible and I need not make other arrangements.

My parachute did open. The landing was not soft. I became entangled in shrouds but I survived. I gather up the details and equipment of the jump hoping there are no more.

About the Author

Grace H. Kaiser practiced medicine in New Holland, a town in eastern Lancaster County, Pennsylvania, for 28 years. She is a native of Bucks County, Pennsylvania, and a graduate of The College of Chestnut Hill, Philadelphia, and The Philadelphia College of Osteopathic Medicine.

Dr. Kaiser became disabled in October 1978, and had to retire from practice. In 1986 her first book *Dr. Frau, A Woman Doctor Among the Amish* was published. She and her husband, Peter Kaiser, live in Phoenix, Arizona. They are the parents of four and grandparents of three.